Messa... Grandad

Dear Sam,

I am writing to you ...

love Grandad

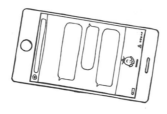

NEWS
TSUNAMI

NEWS
WAR!

Encouragement
for a young
Christian

MESSAGES FROM GRANDAD

David J.
Randall

Hi Grandad, I got your letter! Love Sam

Published by Christian Focus Publications Ltd,

Geanies House, Fearn, Tain, Ross-shire

IV20 1TW, Scotland, UK.

Tel: 01862 871011

Fax: 01862 871699

www.christianfocus.com

email: info@christianfocus.com

Cover design and illustrations by Pete Barnsley (Creative Hoot)

Printed and bound in Glasgow by Bell and Bain

CONTENTS

7th January.. 7

11th January 13

2nd February 19

19th February.. 23

5th March... 29

30th March.. 33

10th April 37

17th April... 41

3rd May 47

12th May 51

4th June.. 57

13th June... 61

27th June... 65

14th July... 69

31st July 75

1st August.. 79

15th August 83

22nd August.. 89

18th September... 95

3rd October 99

16th October 105

1st November.. 111

20th November 117

11th December.. 123

Sam is a young teenager whose family has recently moved from Malawi to the United Kingdom. Sam's parents were missionaries working with the church in Malawi and since their return to the UK, Sam has been settling in to a new school and to a new and more secular culture. This has been a challenge to them all, and, after spending the Christmas holidays with the family, Grandad has been writing to Sam. He wants to do what the apostle Peter did for Silvanus when he encouraged him to stand firm in the grace of God (1 Peter 5:12) and to be able to give a response to the things people say about Christianity (1 Peter 3:15).

7th January
Dear Sam,

We enjoyed our time with you and the family recently, and now that you're back in this country, Granny and I should be able to see more of you. This last Christmas must have

seemed very different from the ones you celebrated in Africa – including the weather; last year it would be sunshine and warmth, but not this year. And I believe the people in Malawi maybe get nearer to the real meaning of Christmas than many people in our culture where Santa and his reindeer seem to get more attention than the baby Jesus.

I know you've joined the Scouts, and I remember a Scout Gang Show where there was a sketch based on the characters of Charles Dickens. Someone was dressed up as Scrooge and he came on stage with his Bah-Humbugs. Somebody else was meant to be David Copperfield, and of course there had to be Oliver Twist who was always asking for more.

These characters were acting out their parts and then an unknown character came on stage. They asked who he was and he answered, "I'm Charles Dickens, the one who created all of you." The sketch ended with the others saying "Never heard of him", and the Dickens character saying to himself, "Fancy – all these people and they don't know the one who created them."

It was a good sketch; it might have been called a parable, because something similar might be said about Jesus' life in this world. Many didn't recognise the One through whom (as John 1:3 says) everything came into existence. I'm afraid that, as you're discovering, there are many people in this country who don't know or care about their Creator who came to the world. So I can understand that, coming back from a land where so many do follow Jesus, you'll be having a hard time adjusting to life here.

I remember you saying that it hasn't been easy to settle into school life since you started at the Academy in August. When we were out walking on Boxing Day, you told me about some of the things you've heard people saying – things that are supposed to be reasons for rejecting "religion", and since then I've been wondering about whether we could continue that discussion by correspondence. Of course I would encourage you to discuss things with your mum and dad, but now that I'm retired I've got all the time in the world! You're probably into all kinds of social media, and while I stick to letters, I'm happy if you respond any way you like.

Maybe we could think about some things that might help to strengthen your faith and help you to have some answers to the things people say about Christianity. What about making it a New Year's resolution to write every few weeks, and see if we can keep it up through the year.

One of the things you said is that it's not just other pupils but sometimes teachers who criticise Christianity – like your physics teacher who called people stupid if they believe that God made the world. He wasn't exactly wise in asking for that show of hands of those who "still" (as he put it) believe in a Creator God. I'm glad you had the courage to put your hand up, along with a few others, even if some people did call you names in the corridor afterwards. "Of course, little Sam still goes to church" is hardly a very intelligent view of such things.

When I was young it wasn't always easy to follow Jesus, but I'm sure it's much harder for you now. So many people see religion and Christianity as old-fashioned, out-of-date, something you grow out of. And so many concentrate on "things" – being rich, successful or famous – rather than God and regard people who believe in God and go to church as a bit weird.

I know you read quite a few children's books when you were younger, but I'm sure there's no danger of you falling into the trap of getting stuck at an infant level, like some teenagers who imagine that because they've grown out of such books ("I've had all I can take of David and Goliath") they can leave Christianity behind with the tooth fairy.

And when it comes to answering the things people throw at you, here are a few things we should remember about believing in Jesus and following Him:

• One is that there are many things we don't know. It would be terrible if people (grandparents included!) acted as if we were know-alls. We don't know all the answers. But that doesn't mean that we don't know *any* answers and I hope I can help you to have answers to some of the things people say.

• We also believe that a time will come when all questions will be answered – when we see Jesus face to face. For the moment – well, in the last letter he wrote, Paul referred to the

trials that had come to him because of his faith in Jesus and he wrote, "But I am not ashamed, for I know whom I have believed" (2 Timothy 1:12). There were things he didn't understand and perhaps questions even he couldn't answer, but he was sure that he was trusting a Lord who does have the answers.

• We should also remember that no amount of argument will make anyone a Christian. Do you know the hymn, *Amazing Grace.* The story of the hymn is an amazing story because its writer, John Newton, was once a wild man living an ungodly life. But in the hymn about his conversion, he said that it was "grace that taught my heart to fear and grace my fears relieved". What did he mean? Well, Jesus once said to His disciples, "You did not choose me, but I chose you" (John 15:16) – that's what John Newton realised. When people become Christians they increasingly realise that it's down to God's Spirit calling them and drawing them to trust in Jesus.

• The other thing to remember is that it's not likely any time soon to become easier to stand up for Jesus. Jesus never said it would be easy. He even said, "If they persecute me, they will also persecute you" (John 15:20). The persecution may be in a different league from what Christians face in some parts of the world, but for us too – well, commitment to Jesus isn't going to make you popular with everybody.

The Bible says nobody should harm you if you stand up for what is right, but if you do suffer in any way because you follow Jesus, you will be blessed by God. It says: "Have no fear of them, nor be troubled, but in your hearts honour Christ the Lord as holy, always being prepared to make a defence to anyone who asks you for a reason for the hope that is in you." (1 Peter 3:13-15)

Let me finish this first letter by referring to the story of Daniel in the Bible.

The book of Daniel starts with Daniel's clear decision to follow God's way wherever he was and whatever it would cost. By the time he faced the lions he would have been elderly, but the story starts when he was probably a teenager.

He was one of many prisoners deported to Babylon (in today's Iraq). At first, things went really well for him. He was selected for special training for the Babylonian civil service. But there was a problem about the food served to Daniel and his friends. We don't know all the details but perhaps it had been dedicated in the name of pagan gods.

And maybe that's why "Daniel resolved that he would not defile himself with the king's food." It wasn't that he'd gone veggie! It was a sign of his loyalty to his God. And maybe you know the story – how he and his friends fared better on their chosen diet than others who (as we say) ate royally.

King Nebuchadnezzar had already tried to lead them away from their commitment to the Lord. With us, names don't usually mean much. I don't know if that's true in Africa where you grew up, but here – well, one of your cousins is called George. That means farmer, but I don't think his parents were trying to choose a career for him.

But in Bible times, names often did mean something, and the "el" part of Daniel's name means God. By changing his name (to Belteshazzar) the king was trying to cut God (el) out of his life. Bel was the name of one of the (many) Babylonian gods, and Nebuchadnezzar wanted to turn him away from El and make him a worshipper of Bel.

But, whatever name Daniel/Belteshazzar had, he resolved (as it says) not to defile himself. It wasn't like the New Year resolutions that people sometimes joke about; somebody makes a resolution to be kinder to their brother or sister, or get up earlier in the morning – but they've forgotten all about it by January the tenth.

Daniel's resolution did last. He did what Ecclesiastes 12:1 says: "Remember your Creator in the days of your youth". Of course "remember" doesn't mean thinking about past events. It's about trusting and honouring the Lord here and now.

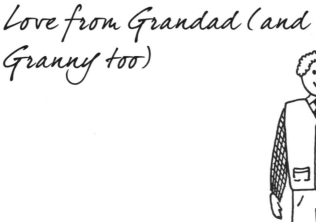

That chapter goes on to some of the things that afflict people of my age – hearing not so good, not sleeping so well, and so on. I'm so glad to know that you want to "remember" Him now, not just when you're old like me!

Let me know how you're getting on, and whether you're up for this plan of a New Year resolution to keep in touch.

Love from Grandad (and Granny too)

11th January

Dear Sam,

I was delighted to get your message this morning; I didn't expect to hear from you so soon and maybe we'll struggle to keep up this early pace!

Thanks for making that list of things you've heard people say. I've added some others to make a kind of "syllabus" for our communications.

1. "How can you believe in God when so many horrible and wicked things happen in the world?"

2. "Religion has caused a lot of war and fighting and we'd be better off without it."

3. "Science has disproved the Bible."

4. "The Bible is full of contradictions."

5. "You only believe because that's the way you were brought up."

6. "You're weird for not being willing to do some things on a Sunday."

7. "Having sex with someone isn't that big a deal."

8. "Families come in all shapes and sizes now, and it's up to you whether you link up with or marry someone of the opposite or the same sex."

9. "It's OK to believe in Jesus privately if you must, but other people follow other religions and nobody can say which is the right one."

10. "I know people who are supposed to be Christians but they aren't very good or attractive people."

11. "If you need a crutch, go ahead, but we can manage fine without religion."

12. "Christianity is just wishful thinking."

13. "What really matters is achieving as much money, success or fame as possible."

That should keep us going for some time.

I sympathise with what you wrote, by the way, about sometimes feeling tongue-tied – you just can't get the words out right and afterwards you think of what you might have said. I think we've all felt like that at times.

The Bible says we should always be ready to "make a defence to anyone who asks you for a reason for the hope that is in you; yet do it with gentleness and respect." (1 Peter 3:13-15)

It was Peter who wrote that down, but he wasn't always ready to do it himself, was he? We read about him saying three times over that he didn't know anything about Jesus of Nazareth, and the story ends with: "He began to invoke a curse on himself and to swear, 'I do not know the man of whom you speak.' And immediately the cock crowed a second time. And Peter remembered how Jesus had said to him, 'Before the cock crows twice, you will deny me three times.' And he broke down and wept." (Mark 14:71-72)

They say "big boys don't cry" – which is rubbish really – but I shouldn't think Peter wept very often. But that night he was a broken man; he realised that he had messed up. He once said he would rather die than let Jesus down, but all it took was the simple question of a servant girl, and big strong Peter fell.

But think of this: how do we know that story? Scholars believe that Mark was the first of the four gospels to be written down and that Mark got much of his information from Peter. And, instead of wanting the storied buried, perhaps it was Peter who insisted that the sad tale should be included – for the sake of honesty and also as an encouragement to others who have failed.

I remember hearing of a legend (it's not in the Bible) which says that when some people saw Peter passing by they would mockingly cup their hands over their mouths and say, "Cock-a-doodle-doo". Some people like to rub other people's noses in their failures.

And how would Peter respond, do you think? My guess is that he might have gone over to them and said, "Yes, it's true; I did deny Him – but He has forgiven me and given me a new start." And we know that Peter became the leader of the early church.

And when he was trying to strengthen believers for times of trial and persecution, it's as if he says, "Don't be like me me that night; I wasn't ready, but I was forgiven and I learned from my downfall."

As a Scout you know the motto, "Be prepared". That's what Peter says.

But how? Before we come to the objections people offer, it's worth thinking about the guidance we find in the Bible about how to react if people laugh at us.

• First, it says – be **respectful**. After Peter's words about being ready to give a reason for your faith, he adds, "do it with gentleness and respect." There's no use shouting at people or trying to force them to believe.

• We should be **honest**. You wrote about sometimes not knowing what to say. Well none of us knows all the answers about God and the Bible. When you think about it, if we could understand everything about God, we'd be as clever as He is! In Star Wars, Yoda called arrogance "a flaw more and more common among Jedi. Too sure of themselves they are." We don't want that.

• Thirdly, we are to be **confident**. Christianity isn't afraid of people asking difficult questions or even doubting. Some of the people in the Bible (for example in the Psalms) expressed doubts, and God is big enough to take it!

• The Bible also says be **strong**. When Joshua was taking over leadership from Moses (which must have been a daunting prospect), God's message to him was: "Be strong and courageous. Do not be frightened, and do not be dismayed, for the Lord your God is with you wherever you go." (Joshua 1:9)

• And lastly we are to be **gracious**. After all, our aim isn't to win arguments but to point people towards believing in God too.

You've had the advantage of being brought up to believe in God and follow Jesus, and I know what you mean about thinking your story's pretty tame. I've also read books and been at meetings where people speak about amazing things that happened and how they were dramatically changed ("converted").

Like you, I've "always believed." I was taken to Sunday School (as we called it then;

they mostly have trendier names nowadays) and taught the things of God. I can't really remember a time when I didn't believe in God. Like Timothy in the Bible, I've known from infancy the Scriptures which make us wise for salvation through faith in Christ Jesus (2 Timothy 3:15). For me there wasn't any dramatic change, so you're not alone in feeling your story isn't very dramatic.

Remember C. S. Lewis's *The Lion, the Witch and the Wardrobe*. Lewis himself was brought up to believe in God, but he rejected Christianity and called himself an atheist.

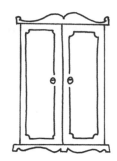

Various things led to a change of heart, and he likened it to waking up. You've been asleep and then gradually you realise that you're awake. I'm not talking about days when you have to set the alarm so that you're up in time to get breakfast and still catch the school bus. But in the holidays or on a Saturday; sometimes you couldn't say, "I woke up at 7.27 this morning" (or is it 9.27!) – but you certainly know that you were asleep and now you are awake. For some people, coming to faith is a bit like that.

Your story is your story, however God has led you, just as my testimony, tame as it may seem, is my testimony. God has different ways of dealing with people. The important thing is to know that we have asked Him into our lives as our Saviour and we are growing in faith.

Let me end for now with an excerpt from another of the Narnia stories, *Prince Caspian*, where there's this conversation between Aslan the lion (who represents Jesus) and Lucy.

"Welcome, child," he said.

"Aslan," said Lucy, "you're bigger."

"That is because you are older, little one," answered he.

"Not because you are?"

"I am not. But every year you grow, you will find me bigger."

That's what I've found as I've grown older – not just in years (don't rub it in!) – but older in faith. I've found over and over again that God grows bigger – not because He has changed, but because I have grown through my reading of the Bible and sharing in the church's worship. I hope the same will be true for you.

Some things belong to childhood and need to be left behind as you grow up (like the tooth fairy and Santa Claus). But faith in Jesus is not one of them.

I'll look forward to hearing from you.

Grandad

P.S. You'll notice that I usually include Bible references (normally from the English Standard Version) for verses I quote so that, if you want, you can check them out for yourself.

2nd February
Dear Sam,

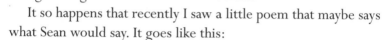

Thanks for your message with all your news. I was on the phone to your dad and he seems to think you're settling in OK at school. He mentioned that you'd been speaking about your friend, Sean, who says he doesn't believe in God at all, and I thought I might write about that this time.

It so happens that recently I saw a little poem that maybe says what Sean would say. It goes like this:

I mean, what
What if no-one's watching
What if when we're dead
I mean, what
What if it's just us down here
What if God is just an idea
Someone put in your head

How can we answer people like Sean? How do we know there is a God in the first place?

You might expect that to be the subject of page one of the Bible, but it isn't. It just starts with, "In the beginning, God created the heavens and the earth."

Still, the Bible does give plenty of evidence for His existence. There's creation, there's conscience and there's Christ – three Cs (you'd never guess I'm a preacher, would you?)

First, there's the evidence of creation. A famous atheist called Bertrand Russell was asked what he would say if, to his surprise, he found himself in front of God. He said he'd tell God that He

hadn't given enough evidence. Well, the Bible says that God has given plenty of evidence of His existence in the things He has created.

In Romans Paul wrote about God's "eternal power and divine nature" being seen "ever since the creation of the world, in the things that have been made" (Romans 1:20).

There's also Psalm 19 which says that the heavens declare the glory of God. Have you had the experience of being (as we say) blown away by the beauty and order of the world around us. It might be a sunrise in Africa, a mountain view in Scotland or the intricate beauty of something as common as the flowers in your garden. There is so much beauty and order in the world that it's hard to think it could all have come about by chance.

Suppose you went to the beach one day and found that your name was written in the sand. You would know that somebody had been there writing with a stick. Nobody could ever convince you that the writing "just happened" by chance. Well, if that's so, how much more when you think about the greatness and the glory of all of creation.

As you know, your uncle Tom is an eye doctor (ophthalmologist to you and me), and if you were to ask him about the eyes with which you're reading this, he'd go on for ages and ages about how amazing our eyes are. He once tried to explain it to me and I wrote some of it down. The small retina in each eye contains about 130 million rod-shaped cells which detect light and send impulses to the brain through about a million nerves, and nearly six million cells see the differences in colours. The eyes are kept clean by ducts which produce the right amount of liquid and our eyelids wipe our eyes clean in one five-hundredth of a second. He once said to me, "Dad, such an amazing result couldn't have come about by some chance of evolution."

When I was at school, we read some of the plays of Shakespeare, and one of his most famous quotes (it's in *Hamlet*) is, "What a piece of work is a man!" That's true (you'll probably say the same goes for females), and yet some people will try to convince you that we're just collections of atoms, shaped by our genes, and our only purpose is to ensure the survival of the species.

Sometimes people think they've got us stumped when they come up with the FAQ, "You say God made everything, but who made God?"

But there's no need to be floored by that one. If God had been made by someone or something else, he wouldn't be God, would He? We could define God as the uncreated Creator of everything else – so that "Who created the One who is uncreated?" becomes a silly question. It's a bit like asking "How heavy is purple?" The question doesn't make sense.

The fact that God has always existed may baffle our minds – but how could it be otherwise? God is bound to be beyond our understanding. Even in this created world there are many things we can't understand (your big sister Tracey says she has fallen in love – who can explain a thing like that) – never mind times when we're talking about Almighty God.

On that happy note, I'll sign off for now; I've got an appointment for a blood test. Next time I'll write about the other two Cs.

Love from us both,
Grandad

19th February
Dear Sam,

So your big sister got a Valentine's card last week. Your turn will come!

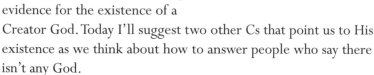

I hope my last letter was helpful. Creation itself is strong evidence for the existence of a Creator God. Today I'll suggest two other Cs that point us to His existence as we think about how to answer people who say there isn't any God.

If creation is one kind of evidence, **conscience** is another. Where does our sense of right and wrong come from?

There are some rules which only apply in certain parts of the world. In this country, for example, the maximum speed limit on motorways is 70 mph, but it may be different in other countries (so watch out if you're travelling abroad once you pass your test).

But there are other rules that seem to be pretty well universal. You might say it's self-evident that people shouldn't tell lies or murder other people. But how do we know that such things are wrong?

It's because God has given us a conscience. We are often tempted to ignore our conscience and do wrong things anyway, but we still "just know" what is right; conscience is like the needle of a compass that points to what is right.

It's true that conscience can be misled; it needs to be moulded by what God has revealed in the Bible. But yes, there is a voice that tells us when we've done wrong — we talk about having "a bad conscience about it". It's not just the fear of punishment or the fear of what other people will think of us. There's something in us that disturbs our conscience when we do wrong, and this too is evidence that there is a God. Otherwise, where would such concerns come from?

Ecclesiastes 3:11 brings together these first two evidences for God's existence when it says, "God has made everything beautiful in its time" and "Also, he has put eternity into man's heart", so that we are incomplete without faith in God.

Mind you, all of this so far still leaves us with the question of what God is like. It's all very well to consider the evidence that something exists, and some people talk vaguely about "a higher power" or "the man in the sky". Other people think of Him as a kind of heavenly tyrant who's always trying to catch you out.

One minister said that when people told him they didn't believe in God, he would sometimes reply, "Tell me what sort of a God you don't believe in." And often the other person had a strange picture of God, and the minister would end up saying, "I don't believe in that God either!"

Anyway, creation and conscience are strong evidences for the existence of God.

And, of course, the third C is **Christ**. Remember the hymn you learned years ago (I don't know if you learned it in English or in Chichewa) that says, "Jesus loves me, this I know, for the Bible tells me so."

When one of your uncles was little, he would sometimes ask lots of questions – little children are famous for that. Once he was asking about his body and who made him. His mum thought he was too young to explain about how babies are made, and she simply said God had made him. He'd been learning that hymn and so his next question was, "Is that the God of *Jesus loves me?*"

Well, that's exactly what Christians believe – the God who created everything and put eternity in our hearts is "the God of *Jesus loves me.*"

This is the most important thing of all. God has come into this world in Jesus Christ who was fully divine and fully human. He is the subject of the whole Bible. What we call the Old Testament prepared the way for His coming, the four gospels (Matthew, Mark, Luke and John) tell of His life, teaching and ministry, and the rest of the New Testament draws out the meaning of what He said and did.

C. S. Lewis (of Narnia fame) wrote a famous passage about how there are three possible views of Jesus.

- People could say He was mad and the disciples were simpletons who believed His nonsense.

- Or they could say He was bad – which may sound surprising because most people would say that Jesus was a really good man. But Lewis was thinking of the kind of things Jesus said – for example, "Anyone who has seen me has seen God" (John 14:9). Anybody who goes around saying things like that – well, if he's not mad and if it isn't true, that person is wicked – putting about ridiculous stories to gain a following. (Most of those who do anything like that, do it to make themselves rich, and that's a problem for people who say Jesus was just a good man – because, as we know, He didn't have any worldly possessions.)

- The other option is that Jesus was God, as He said Himself, as the Bible teaches and as His people have believed all through the centuries.

These were the three options Lewis put forward: mad, bad or God. And the challenge is: read the accounts of Jesus' life in the four gospels and see what impression they make on you. Is it credible that He was mad or bad – or do His words and actions show Him to be who He claimed to be, God in the flesh (incarnate is the big word for it)?

There are three ways of answering the question about God's existence: creation, conscience and Christ all point us to a God in heaven.

And we could add the evidence of changed lives through the centuries. There have been many many people whose lives were going haywire, who were doing wrong things and causing trouble for other people, until they came to believe in Jesus, and then their lives were changed. Paul was one example. He once hated even the

name of Jesus, but his whole life was changed when he met the risen Jesus on the road to Damascus (the story is told in Acts 9).

So, where have we got to? We've thought about the evidence for God (creation, conscience and Christ). But what if people agree that there must be "something" and then say, "But we can never know what that something is like".

The answer is – He has made Himself known to us.

We know about that in human relationships. You've been making new friends since you came back to the U.K., and think of it: if you want to know someone, you can observe some things about that person – whether the person is male or female, slim or well-built, white or brown. But if you really want to know the person, you are dependent on that person's willingness to be known by you. If the person closes up and refuses to reveal anything about himself or herself, there's not much you can do about it. You can't really get to know that person.

And with God – if He didn't want to be known by us, there wouldn't be a lot we could do. But He has revealed Himself to us. As we've seen He has revealed Himself in creation, in conscience and in Christ. We also, of course, have His book, the Bible (we'll come to that another time).

Hope to see you soon.

5th March
Dear Sam,

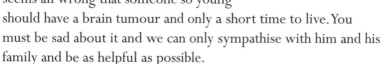

I was really sorry to hear about your
friend Tim and his illness. Somehow it
seems all wrong that someone so young
should have a brain tumour and only a short time to live. You
must be sad about it and we can only sympathise with him and his
family and be as helpful as possible.

And you're right that this is just the sort of thing that people
bring up as a reason for not believing in God. They'll say things
like, "If there were a God and He has the power to stop disease,
why doesn't He?" or "If He is supposed to be a God of love, how
can He let this happen?"

Your message about Tim reminded me of a teenager I used to
visit in Edinburgh. I would climb the stairs to the tenement house
where James lived. I say "lived" but it wasn't much of a life. He
just lay day after day in a sort of cot-like bed, because when he
was a child he had fallen down several flights of stairs and suffered
brain damage. He couldn't do anything for himself, his situation
was a constant strain to his family, and he died
while he was still in his teens. And then there's
also so much suffering and death through war,
famine, tsunamis, diseases, and so on.

Yes, it's one of the commonest objections
to Christian faith and one of the hardest to
answer, but the Christian claim is that
it makes more sense to trust in God
than to reject Him, even when we
don't know all the answers.

Your mum told me you've started keyboard lessons. Well, just suppose Mrs Fraser took hundreds of little cards with the symbol of one musical note on each one. And then, suppose she threw them all up in the air, and then later they were all lying in a way that made a piece of music. Would anyone believe such a thing had happened by chance, that Mr Nobody did it (as little children say)? Of course not. You would know that a musician had been there. Even if there were a few notes that didn't seem to fit very well, that wouldn't stop you believing that a musician had been at work.

And even though things happen that are hard to explain, that doesn't mean that we have to conclude that there can't be a God.

 The Bible tells us that God created everything. The first chapter of the Bible ends with, "God saw everything that he had made, and behold, it was very good" (Genesis 1:31).

But then it goes on to what we call "the Fall". God gave Adam and Eve a choice and they chose to go their own way and rebel against God. This brought sin into the world and the consequences have been disastrous. So much of the world's suffering comes about as a result of human foolishness, ignorance or sin. We have free will and the sad truth is that human beings, in rebellion against God, have used that free will to make whips, guns, bayonets, bombs and so forth.

But then somebody will say, "True, a lot of suffering is caused by human beings, but what about earthquakes and floods?" And we simply don't understand why God allows some of these things; they seem to be "discords". But we can still believe in the Musician (if you follow me). The Bible tells us that God is working out purposes which are unknown to us.

Occasionally, we can actually see positive results from unwelcome events – like Joseph in the Bible who suffered a lot of injustice but later came to recognise that God has been working out His plan (Genesis 50:20). He saw what Paul later would mean about God working in everything for good for those who love Him (Romans 8:28).

Sometimes we see it in ordinary things. I remember the time when your cousin, Emma, wanted to go on a school skiing trip. Her parents weren't very sure about signing the permission slips; they were worried that Emma might get hurt, but eventually they allowed her to go. Did that mean they didn't care about her? Of course not, but we tolerate certain things – even risks – for the sake of a greater good.

Suppose you had never heard of surgical operations and you found yourself looking into an operating theatre where you saw a man in a green overall using knives and other instruments on a helpless patient. You might think it was extreme cruelty, but of course he's a surgeon, and the problem would be your lack of knowledge.

It's often that way – our limited knowledge means we can't see the sense in some things that God allows to happen, but if everything the Bible says about Him is right, then we can trust that He has a good purpose.

There's an example of it in the story of Job. Job suffered a series of calamities – he lost his wealth, his family and his health in quick succession. And yet at the end of the book of Job we find him saying that, through it all, he had come to a stronger faith. That may seem strange, but it has often been like that. Many people have grown stronger through times of trial.

That book of Job also says that people shouldn't torture themselves with the question, "What did I do to deserve this?" There are some things where we are to blame; for example, if you take drugs there may be consequences for your health. But Job had a group of friends who kept saying that he must have done terrible things and he was being punished. It's not so simple as that.

But I've written enough for now. I'll leave some other things till next time.

Grandad

30th March
Dear Sam,

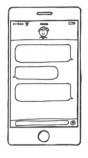

How is Tim these days? It must be a difficult time for everybody and I hope he gets the best of care. I've been praying for him.

Last time I was trying to help with the question of why God allows some awful things to happen in the world. Just this week, I heard of a friend who was in my class at school who was cycling along when a car came out from a junction and hit him. He died at the scene and left all his family and friends in shock.

That last e-mail ended with the question that people sometimes ask: "What did I do to deserve this?" I should have gone on to write about what Jesus said – the Jesus whose sufferings we remember in this so-called holy week.

Once He met a man who was blind and His disciples asked, "Rabbi, who sinned, this man or his parents, that he was born blind?" (John 9:2) Jesus said it's not so simple as that; their equation was wrong. "It was not that this man sinned, or his parents, but that the works of God might be displayed in him." The note in my Study Bible comments, "God sometimes allows people to suffer so that they can experience His mercy and power in delivering them."

Another time, Jesus commented on some events that must have been in the news at the time. Some people from Galilee had been slaughtered by Pontius Pilate, and there was also a fatal accident when a tower fell and killed a number of people. Some people were implying that the residents in these places must have been really bad sinners for such things to happen. And what did Jesus say? He said it wasn't that they were worse sinners than others – although He also warned them that, if they persisted in sin, calamity would eventually come upon them. (Luke 13:1-5)

That's what the Bible says – persistent sin and rebellion will have consequences, but we can't and shouldn't conclude from any particular trouble that the sufferer has done things that deserve that punishment.

I wonder if you've read the story of Joni Eareckson? When she was a teenager Joni had a diving accident that left her paralysed. She suffered a great deal: many operations, suicidal thoughts, and so on. Now, years later, she heads up "Joni and Friends – International Disability Center" which ministers to disabled people. Instead of spending her years complaining and moaning, she testifies to a sense of peace that comes from the Lord. She has even said, "I'd rather be in this wheelchair knowing Him, than on my feet without Him."

Let me include here some words she wrote:

"Sometimes when we ask 'why?', I don't think that we're looking for answers. I don't know that even if we had answers, they would suffice. So when I ask 'Why?' (and sometimes I do ask 'Why?' even now – because of new levels of pain on my shoulders and neck), I'm like the kid who has ridden his bike, fallen off, scraped his knee and looks up at Daddy and says, 'Why, Daddy?' That child doesn't want answers. That child just wants Daddy to pick him up, press him against his breast and say, 'It's going to be OK – Daddy's here'. That's what I want when I say 'Why?'. I just want God to be near and to hold me and say 'I'm not going to leave you'. And that helps."

In another book, *A Lifetime of Wisdom*, she gives this encouraging message:

"When life seems wild, crazy and utterly out of control, it is not. When it seems as though God has forgotten you or turned His back on you to tinker with some other universe, He has not. When it seems like you have somehow fallen out of His favour or missed the bus on His love, you have not. And that's what it means to walk by faith."

That's written by someone who has a right to speak. I mean, it's all very well for someone like me – flu is about the worst thing I've had – but Joni is different; she knows what she's talking about.

I hope my last letter and this one will help, as you think about these things. We can never know all the answers, but suffering doesn't have to be a Stop sign on the road of faith. It makes more sense to trust in God, even with our questions, than it would to conclude that there isn't any God.

And by the way, the Bible itself includes many instances of people wrestling with this issue. Many of the Psalms, for example, come from times of suffering and undeserved persecution by enemies. And we don't have to be shy about expressing everything to God in our prayers, even when we're struggling – perhaps especially when we're struggling.

This has been rather a "heavy" letter this time, but, before we leave the subject, there's one other thing to remember: Jesus knows what it is to suffer. In Jesus, God Himself has come right into this world of suffering, and He made a way of salvation through the suffering and death of Jesus. God understands our troubles. He sympathises, and millions of people have found that faith in Him helps them get through difficult experiences.

Has your church sung Graham Kendrick's song about it? It's based on the words of Hebrews 4:14-16, and it says:

He walked where I walk,
He stood where I stand,
He felt what I feel –
He understands.

Some of the other religions in the ancient world would say to people, "Don't worry – the gods won't be bothered about little you". The Bible says the God who is real does care about little you.

It also promises that a time will come when all of our questions will be answered, a time when there will be no more death, mourning, crying or pain (Revelation 21:4), a time when the picture will be complete.

I can hardly expect that this letter has answered all the questions you might be asked about this subject. If you want to think more about it, I could suggest some books and DVDs for you to look at. But in the end of the day we just don't know all the answers. But, as I said earlier, it still makes more sense to trust in God even when it's tough than to reject the way of faith.

Sunday coming will be Easter and I hope you have a wonderful time. On Friday we'll remember what Jesus went through for our salvation, and then Sunday is a great day of joy as we celebrate His victory. That's much more wonderful than chocolate eggs – but I hope you enjoy them too.

Love from us both,
Grandad

10th April
Dear Sam,

Well, how many Easter eggs did you get? Isn't chocolate good! I guess Easter here would seem a little different from last Easter when you were still in Malawi, but of course the message is the same all over the world: the stone was rolled away – the Lord is risen.

We've been thinking about suffering as a major reason many people give for not believing in God. Another, is the idea that "religion" has been the cause of an awful lot of conflict and war and we'd be better off without it.

Often it goes along with the view that there is no God anyway and Christianity is a thing of the past. Things like that may be said with anger or with calm reason – but it leads many young people (as you'll know better than I do) to question the things they've been taught in church and home, and even wonder whether the atheists are going to win the day.

I know from what you've written that in school you encounter people who tell you such things: the Bible can't be trusted, Christianity is a thing of the past, it's only for young children and old people.

And such doubts may be fanned by the sight, in many parts of this country, of church buildings that were once used for worship but they've been turned into something else (flats, stores, restaurants or whatever). People who come from where you used to live in Malawi

find that hard to understand; they're more concerned to put up additional church buildings. Here, I suppose it's partly that we had far too many church buildings (as a result of past splits and divisions), but unfortunately it gives the impression of a dying religion when church buildings lie derelict or are used for some other purpose.

However, it certainly isn't true that either religion in general or Christianity in particular is dying out. One scholar has suggested that much of the loudness of modern atheists (on TV, in magazines, in classrooms) is what he calls a backlash. They thought they were winning, but now they realise that across the world more people than ever follow some religion. They don't like that – and is that why they make so much noise?

Here in the U.K. many people in education and in the media would tell us that Christianity belongs to a pre-scientific age

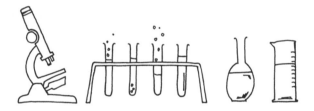

before things like space travel, the digital revolution and genetic engineering.

So far as school is concerned, as you are finding out, many people want to get everything to do with Christianity out of schools – even though it was through Christianity that schools were developed in the first place. And as you go through the school years, you'll probably have less and less Christian teaching and more and more anti-Christian ideas thrown at you.

Sometimes that's because it suits people to reject faith in God. I mean, you've been taught about right and wrong from your earliest days; some things are right and some things are wrong. Much of that teaching would be based on the teaching of Jesus and the Bible, and one reason why many people want to get rid of religion is that it leaves them free to do whatever they want, without being held back by ideas of right and wrong.

For example, a famous atheist called Aldous Huxley (most famous for his book, *Brave New World*) admitted openly that he wanted to believe there is no God. He wanted to be free to do what he wanted without any fear of God or judgment; he admitted that's why he became an atheist.

There's a contemporary writer with the wonderful name of Dinesh D'Souza who wrote a book called *What's So Great About Christianity?* Good question – and as we think about it, there are two things to consider. First there's the charge that "religion" has caused so much warfare and suffering in the world, and then the idea that Christianity hasn't really done much good for the world. Let me take up the first today and leave the other till next time.

Sadly, it's just a fact that there have been many so-called religious wars. People have sometimes done terrible things to each other in the name of religion or even in the name of Christ. You may hear people refer to the inquisition, the crusades, slavery and other ways in which people have abused religion (that's the point we're going to emphasise) to cause suffering and pain.

The truth is that these things say more about human prejudice, sinfulness and stupidity than they say about God. The way of Jesus is the way of love, and an enormous amount of good has been done because people have sought to follow His way. When people do bad things in the name of religion, that isn't God's fault.

I kept a cartoon I once saw in a newspaper. It showed a man standing at the complaints desk of a store holding up a pair of football boots. What was his complaint? "They don't shoot straight." Do you think he got his money back? Hardly; the problem wasn't the boots but the wearer. And that's the problem in the bigger things we're considering here.

Or think of science. Do we blame science for many of the horrible things which have resulted from the use of science? Advances in science and technology have given us phones and I-pads and so on, but they have also been used to cause terrible suffering. For example, science enabled the development of napalm, a gel that sticks to human flesh and burns people horribly. But we don't blame science – the problem is with the way people use it. According to a well-known saying, the heart of the problem is the problem of the heart.

And it's to save and help people that Jesus came. Bad things done in the name of religion or of Christianity are done not because Christianity is Christianity, but because human beings are human beings – apt to spoil everything. That has sadly been the story of mankind all along.

On that cheery note I'll stop for today; next time I'll take up the other side of the coin: has Christianity been good for the world?

Hope everybody's fine there.

Grandad

17th April
Dear Sam,

I thought I'd better write a bit sooner than usual so that we don't lose the thread of where we were going last week. We were thinking about what can be said to people who allege that "religion" has caused warfare and suffering and been used (abused, really) to persecute other people.

The other question is: has Christianity done anything positively good for the world? It's the question posed in the title of the book I mentioned, *What's so great about Christianity?*"

That question could be answered by referring to the message of the gospel which is great, and we'll get to that later, but for now let's think about the impact of Christianity on the world.

The very fact that we can ask such questions is amazing when you think about it. I mean, we're talking about someone who lived in Judea a long time ago and who was executed as an alleged rebel against Rome.

Yet His influence on the world has been enormous. There's a statement that goes around in various forms about the influence of Jesus. Here's how it goes:

He was born in an obscure village, the child of a peasant woman. He grew up in another village where he worked in a carpenter's shop until he was thirty. He never went to university, never wrote a book, never held public office. He never travelled more than two hundred miles from the place where He was born.

When He was only thirty-three, He was attacked and killed. His friends ran away and one of them even denied knowing Him. He was handed over to His enemies, went through a mockery of a trial and was nailed to a cross between two criminals. As He died, soldiers gambled for His clothes, the only property He had. He was laid in a borrowed tomb through the pity of a friend.

And yet, all the armies that ever marched, all the parliaments that ever sat, all the kings that ever reigned, put together, have not affected the life of mankind on earth as much as that one solitary life.

It's true – the life, the teaching, the gospel of Jesus has had an enormous impact on the world and it has been a tremendously positive impact. We said last time that God can hardly be held responsible for the errors human beings make, but what is also true is that Christ has inspired His people to do amazing things and through them has brought about many changes for the better.

I don't suppose you've heard of Dr Grenfell and Dr Hunt, two scholars who were examining the results of an archaeological dig in Egypt. They found things that had lain under the sand for centuries, including some crocodile carcases. One of the workmen flung a pick at one of the carcases and the skin cracked. Inside they found some letters.

One of the most interesting ones was a letter from a soldier who was away from home, written to his wife who was expecting a baby. The letter said, "We are still in Alexandria. As soon as I get wages, I will send some. When you have the baby, the best of luck. If it's a boy, let it alone; if it's a girl, throw it away."

Can you believe anyone could be so callous and cruel? We recognise that male and female are equally important and we find a letter like that shocking. Attitudes have changed and anyone who expressed such a thing today would be howled down (well, not everybody, because a huge number of babies are aborted nowadays and we even hear of sex-selective abortion – all harking back to a kind of pre-Christian outlook).

But the truth is that many things which we take for granted have come about because of Jesus (even the holidays you've just been enjoying – originally holy days). It was Christianity that developed hospitals and schools, and many examples could be given of how Christ's influence has led to wonderfully positive gains for mankind.

- Think of William Wilberforce campaigning for the end of the slave trade
- Lord Shaftesbury pioneering the care of needy children
- or Elizabeth Fry fighting for prison reform

- One of my boyhood heroes was David Livingstone – explorer, doctor and missionary – who did so much for Africa (including the country in which you lived for most of your life so far)
- It was in obedience to God's call that Mary Slessor left the slums of Dundee to go to Nigeria where, among others things, she put an end to the abandonment of twins. People feared that the father of one of the infants was an evil spirit, and, since they couldn't tell which one, they would often abandon both babies in the bush.

By the way, it has become trendy to imply that such missionaries had bad motives; David Livingstone, for example, has been criticised for aiding European powers to gain wealth out of Africa, or they say he was more of an explorer than a missionary. It's not fair to attack people who can't now defend themselves, but people like Livingstone were motivated above  all by a desire to help people in every way possible and to tell them the good news of the love of Christ.

Industrialists, explorers, doctors, scientists – there's a long list of people who have responded to the love of God by seeking to help their fellow human beings. And the list of organisations that have been founded through Christian compassion is a long one. To name a few that come to mind:

The Leprosy Mission
Mercy Ships
The Salvation Army
Samaritan's Purse
Evangelical Alliance Relief (Tear) Fund
Christian Aid
Compassion International
World Relief
The Samaritans
Prospects
Blythswood Care (shoe boxes)
Barnardo's Homes
Mission to Fishermen
One that is dear to my heart is the Raven Trust; you'll be

interested in it because it's all about sending aid to Malawi. The Trust has sent over a hundred 40-foot containers to help Malawian people; I think you saw one being unloaded in Malawi.

I expect you could find out more about these (and many other) Christian organisations if you put their names into a search engine. Clearly, it's not only Christians who care for others, but actually we don't often hear of atheists' relief agencies, orphanages, hospitals or charities, whereas the influence of Jesus Christ has made an enormous difference to the world.

And still today the Christian church is the largest provider of healthcare and education in the world, especially in poor countries. In 2013, a British member of parliament spoke of how churches provide almost 100 million hours of unpaid voluntary work on social projects every year, and, despite what we hear about the economic situation, church members alone have increased their donations to social action projects by 19% in two years to £342 million. She went on to speak of Britain's reliance on churches to meet social needs through the running of food banks, homework clubs, street patrols, and so on.

It all helps to give an answer to the question, "What good has Christianity done for the world?"

At its heart is its central message, which is that God loved the world so much that He sent His Son into the world – Jesus Christ who lived, taught, loved, died and rose again – so that whoever believes in him should not perish but have everlasting life (John 3:16).

We'll have more to say about that later, but next time I'll turn to another objection people make – you've mentioned it before: the idea that science has killed off faith. Obviously, of course, it hasn't, but there is the belief, or at least suspicion, that science and faith are like oil and water – they don't mix. But that's a subject for another day.

I guess the school holidays are over now; back to the grindstone.

Granny and I send our love to all the family.

Grandad

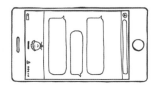

3rd May
Dear Sam,

Thanks for your text about looking forward to getting some help with the science/faith question. It's often said – that modern science makes it impossible to believe any longer in God or the Bible.

That brings us back to Dr Jones, your physics teacher (aka "Indiana", I believe!) I gather he keeps saying that scientific advance means nobody can believe in God any longer – or at least people are stupid if they do. I suppose he would grant that Christianity has some historical interest, but he thinks that science has buried God.

Much that we hear in the media takes the same idea for granted; some popular TV programmes make bold statements about the natural world that just assume there's no God behind it all. That's one of the issues we face, even although many scientists today do believe in God.

It's all about attitudes – sometimes called people's worldview. Many people have adopted a worldview that excludes all thought of God from the very start. It's not that they've thought things out and come to a reasoned conclusion about faith or no faith. They just assume that only idiots (if they're being unkind) or uneducated people (if they're a bit gentler) have faith in an unseen God.

And how do we form our outlook? I was interested to see a newspaper report the other day about the internet. A survey had shown that many young people think that anything they read on the internet must be true.

People used to joke about not believing everything you read in the newspapers – but these findings are quite worrying.

The report suggested that one in five people between ages twelve and fifteen accept whatever they find on the web. Sometimes adults think that kids now have more savvy than ever, but this report suggests that many are rather naïve. Social media may be useful and enjoyable (though it's a foreign land to older people like me), but you need to be careful.

And what about the assessment that the average young person between ages eight and fifteen spends about fifteen hours a week glued to the internet. I hope that's not true of you.

But that was by the way. The basic problem is that some people who say they believe in science are really believers in scientism. What is scientism? It's an attitude that sees everything only in light of what we can see and touch and experience; it has no time for unseen realities such as we find in the Bible.

I've even heard it described as "nothing buttery": things are "nothing but" a collection of atoms, our bodies are nothing but skin, flesh and bones. We can only hope that people who think like that don't actually treat their family and friends accordingly!

But it's time we got to the basic question. Is it possible to take a scientific view of things and also believe in God?

Of course it is. Christians believe that God is the Maker of everything and that all truth is His, so every scientific discovery should increase our sense of wonder at creation and its Creator. This is God's world and the more we discover about it, the more we can praise its Maker. Life comes from God and the more we discover about life, the more we can worship and love the Giver of life.

Let me refer to some famous scientists:

• The Scottish scientist, Lord Kelvin, once said, "If you think strongly enough, you will be forced by science to believe in God."

• Louis Pasteur (for whom we can be thankful every time we take a drink of milk) said, "Science brings us nearer to God."

• Sir Isaac Newton (discoverer of the law of gravity) claimed that the most beautiful system of the sun, planets and comets could only have come from "the dominion of an intelligent and powerful being".

• And Albert Einstein stated his view that everyone who "is seriously engaged in the pursuit of science becomes convinced that the laws of nature show the existence of someone vastly superior to men."

One of the things often overlooked by those who mock Christianity in the name of science is that science actually owes its origin to Christianity. People became scientific because they looked for order ("laws of nature"), and they did so because they believed in a Law-giver.

As Psalm 19 says, "The heavens declare the glory of God". And, as part of His creation, God has "planted eternity" in us human beings (Ecclesiastes 3:11) – which means that we will never be satisfied or fulfilled by concentrating everything on this world and material things.

That's something that many people have found, like one comedian who used to be very popular. Before there were all the channels there are now, 30 per cent of the people in Britain watched his programme. It was very funny. What isn't so funny is that the comedian, Tony Hancock, took his own life when he was only forty-four. He brought laughter to many, but somehow he couldn't find anything to make his own life worth living.

That's what you call sad, and although many people do find happiness without believing in God, it's the claim of Christianity that faith in Jesus brings "abundant life" (John 10:10). We are more than just stuff – skin and bones and cells and genes; we also have what is called a soul and Jesus said (Matthew 4:4) that people cannot live by bread alone (material things).

A few years ago I visited a place in Germany called Belsen. It's the site of one of the notorious Nazi concentration camps. Walking around in the August sunshine, it was hard to believe that terrible atrocities had been carried out there, the kind of things you learn about in history lessons about the holocaust.

I was interested therefore to read some words of a psychiatrist called Victor Frankl, who was imprisoned in another of these horrible camps (Auschwitz, perhaps the most notorious of them all). Thinking about his experiences there, he concluded, "The gas chambers of Auschwitz were the ultimate consequence of the theory that man is nothing but the product of heredity and environment". He said he became convinced that such evils came from people who believed in nothing other than physical things and power.

That's an extreme example. Of course, unbelievers often live good and loving lives, but the question of the meaning of life remains and, returning to our theme, science can't answer the most basic questions about our lives: where did we come from, why are we here and where are we going?

But I'll stop there for just now. I apologise if this has been a rather "intellectual" letter. I didn't mean it to be, and the questions we're considering are very important for daily living. More later!

Grandad

12th May
Dear Sam,

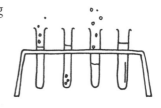

Thanks for the letter you sent with my birthday card last week. I see you still have many questions about science, creation, evolution and so on, and you mentioned also that another of your teachers (ironic when he's the RE teacher) was suggesting that there are many contradictions in the Bible.

Well, Sam, I'm not a scientist and I don't feel qualified to give answers on all the questions you raised. I could suggest some other reading material for you – in fact, maybe I'll add some suggestions in a P.S.

But has science buried God or done away with religion? Well, looking at the world, it obviously hasn't. The United Nations figure for the population of the world is 7.3 billion, and about 7 billion have some of kind of religious belief (mainly Christian, Muslim or Hindu), with only a small number (approximately 0.71 billion) in the non-religious category. The fact that most of the last group seem to live in our western world shouldn't blind us to the fact that science certainly hasn't killed off religion.

But before we get bamboozled with statistics, let's think about what can be said to people who think it has, and that you can't believe the Bible nowadays.

One of the first things to notice is that it's always important to ask the right questions.

As you know from times when you've visited our house, I have loads of books. Looking at the shelves, I see a D.I.Y. manual, the complete works of Robert Burns and (would you believe?) *Alice's Adventures in Wonderland*. What would you say if I complained that Alice's Adventures doesn't say anything about how to put up a shelf, or that Robert Burns doesn't say anything about fixing a dodgy laptop? You'd tell me (politely, I hope) to stop being so silly! You'd tell me that Alice in Wonderland is just a story and Robert Burns had never heard of a laptop. You have to read a book for what it is, not for what it isn't.

Well, that's true of the Bible. It says some things about God creating the world, but it was never meant to be a science textbook. If the Bible had been written in twenty-first century scientific language, most people who've read it would never have been able to understand it.

But if God is the source of all truth, there can't really be any conflict between what is written in the Bible and what science finds out. If there appear to be conflicts, that says more about our lack of understanding than anything else. To put it in a nutshell, science and the Bible don't contradict but complement each other.

In the case of the theory of evolution: when people say that evolution explains everything about life and proves the Bible wrong, they're barking up the wrong tree. Actually, it would be interesting to ask what hard evidence they can produce to make a link between monkeys and humans. Someone has suggested that later ages may be amazed that a theory with so little evidence was accepted by so many for so long.

A friend of mind talks about seeing two people walking along a cliff top when they see a bright red flare shooting up from the sea. One is a scientist who gets out her mobile phone and films it. From her GPS she can calculate some things about the flare and she writes down a full description of what she has seen. The other person is a Scout who says, "That's a distress flare; I must run and tell the coastguard".

Which of them is right? Well, they both gave an accurate account of what they saw. The scientist was working out how it happened; the Scout was working out why it happened. The Bible is mainly concerned with the 'Why?' question – not about flares from out at sea, but about the basic questions of life: where we came from, why we are here and where we are headed.

And a scientific approach to anything uses the proper tools. You don't use Bunsen burners in the modern languages classroom, and you wouldn't use maps or French grammar to study Chemistry. You have to use the appropriate means.

Talking about "scientific" proofs when talking about God is really quite unscientific. When we study French we use the proper methods – vocabulary lists, rules of grammar, and so on; and when we think about God and the Bible, of course we use our brains, but the proper use of our brains is in faith and prayer. Science can do so much, but it has its limitations too.

I love the story I once read about a family of mice that lived inside a piano. Their world was filled with music and they were comforted by the thought that there was an invisible player above them but near them. One day a daring mouse climbed up inside the piano and found out how the music was made. It was all about wires which vibrated and made the musical notes. Later another explorer found that there were hammer-like things that struck the wires. This was a more complicated theory, but it was felt that only ignorant mice could any longer believe in the great player. But, of course, the pianist continued to play.

And if these little mice were having a discussion about how the piano came to exist in the first place, and one of them suggested that it just happened to come together, the others would be sure to say (or should that be squeak?), "Don't be ridiculous".

It's just as ridiculous to say that our amazing universe came about by chance and there is no Creator.

A famous thinker said that if he was walking somewhere and hit his foot on a stone, he might suppose that the stone had lain there for ever. But if he found a watch on the ground, he would hardly think that. He might not know who made it or who lost it, but he would know that somebody had made it and somebody had lost it.

Our universe is an amazingly complex thing, and the more we discover about it, the more we should stand in awe of the One who made it.

So: do we have to choose between believing the Bible and taking a scientific view? Not if we understand what the Bible is (the revealed truth of God) and not if we understand what science is (the study of God's creation).

And before I finish and get to bed, let me refer to the other

thing I brought in at the start – the idea that the Bible is full of contradictions. It has been claimed often and it's tempting to challenge critics by saying, "Well, name one" (often they can't).

In Matthew's account of the Easter story which we read last month, it says "an

angel of the Lord" had rolled back
the stone, and in John's gospel we
read about Mary Magdalene going
to the tomb and "she saw two angels
in white, sitting where the body of

Jesus had been" (John 20:12). If we ask, "Well, which was it then
– one angel or two?" we can easily see that two includes one and
it's simply that Matthew refers to one of them while John refers
to both.

In fact, that kind of thing tells us that the accounts are
accurately written down. What I mean is that if the Bible were
just a made-up story, you'd expect details like this to be made to
fit each other.

What we have in the Bible is not a collection of tall tales and
fables. Luke tells us that he had gone to great pains to investigate
the events surrounding Jesus. He starts off (using Eugene
Peterson's version, *The Message*), by addressing someone called
Theophilus: "Since I have investigated all the reports in close
detail, starting from the story's beginning, I decided to write it
all out for you, so you can know beyond a shadow of a doubt the
reliability of what you were taught."

We can have every confidence in the Bible. It is God's Word,
breathed out by Him and profitable for us (2 Timothy 3:16), and
also it has stood firm against the many attacks that have been
made on it through the ages.

One of the first texts that I learned by heart is Psalm 119:105
– "Your Word is a lamp to my feet and a light to my path." Over
the years I've studied the Bible and preached it thousands of
times, and I think people sometimes wonder how preachers can
keep going Sunday after Sunday, year after year. Well it's because
the Bible is so full and rich. There are always new things to
discover; even if we live to be a hundred we'll never exhaust it.

But I'm not a hundred yet and neither are you. Psalm 119 also says that the best choice you can make while you are young is to live your life according to God's Word (verse 9).

We've been thinking about some attacks on the Bible and I hope what has been written may help you to have confidence in it. But at the end of the day it doesn't need our defence – it can speak for itself. That's what a famous preacher called Charles Spurgeon said when he was asked how he would defend the Bible: "Defend it? I would as soon defend a roaring lion. Let it out. It will defend itself."

Love

Grandad

P.S. I promised I would add a note about some resources to use if you want to pursue these subjects more fully. I'm sure your dad has (or could get) a helpful little booklet by John Blanchard called *Evolution – Fact or Fiction?* I know he does have *Confident Christianity* by Chris Sinkinson (unless he left it in Africa; I sent it for his birthday two years ago); its chapter 8 ("Science Friction") is helpful. Then there's a book which I edited called, *Why I am not an Atheist* (its first chapter is by a scientist who starts with the fascinating comment, "I am a scientist and I think like one. That is one of the main reasons that I am not an atheist.") And lastly, if you go to www.johnlennox.org you'll find a lot of helpful information (John Lennox is a Professor of Maths at Oxford).

4th June
Dear Sam,

Thank you again for the book token you
sent for my birthday. I'll really enjoy
using it.

I was glad to hear that you've joined the Christian Union
group at school. That will help you in your Christian growth, and
your presence will encourage others too.

But it makes me remember another of the things people say
– which is that if you believe in God and belong to any Christian
group, it's only because of the way you were brought up. They
sometimes add, "If you'd been born in India you'd probably be a
Hindu, or if you'd been born in Saudi Arabia you'd probably be a
Muslim." That's one way some people try to more-or-less dismiss
religion.

And at first it sounds like quite a strong argument – what can
we say about it?

The first thing is that the same could be said about
unbelievers. In this country, many people are now brought up
without much (or any) knowledge of Christianity.

That wasn't always true. I was brought up in a Christian
home. We had regular school services and most of my teachers at
least respected Christianity. There used to be church services on
TV and nearly all weddings and funerals were held in church or
conducted by a Christian minister.

But things have changed and some people grow up today with
hardly any knowledge of the Bible and Jesus. I'm sure you hear
people using the name of Jesus and God casually as a swearword.
Often they don't mean to offend, but if you were to ask them

how much they know about Jesus, you'd probably see some blank looks.

Some friends of ours gave one of their children a copy of Richard Scarry's *Best Picture Dictionary Ever*. It's an attractive book, but would you believe it defines Christmas as "a happy holiday, a time for presents and parties and decorating the Christmas tree" and Easter as "a happy holiday in spring, the time for the Easter bunny and for painting Easter eggs." Nothing about Jesus' birth or death and resurrection!

And this argument that you only believe because that's the way you were brought up could be applied to many unbelievers and atheists. Maybe they are only what they are because of the way they were brought up.

But that's not all that can be said about it. We have to agree that our upbringing does have an effect on what we are and sometimes what we believe.

Some people rebel against the teaching they've been given – I'm sure you know some people who were brought up to go to church or Sunday School and then, perhaps in their teenage years, they've turned against Christianity. But for those who are believers, their upbringing may indeed have something to do with it.

I was taken to Sunday School when I was very young (I'm told I cried the first time I was left there on my own – that's my confession for today) and my parents brought me up to believe in Jesus, pray to Him, and so on, and I am thankful for that. In fact, I wish that more children and young people had the same advantage.

But I had to make up my own mind what I believed. That's true for everyone: however we were brought up, we have to decide for ourselves what we believe and what we will stand for.

The main thing for us all is not the question of how we were brought up but the question of truth. We have to decide: which religion expresses the truth about God? It's not just about feelings, or even about what "turns you on" (as people say). Faith in Jesus does result in peace and fulfilment in life, but that's not the main thing.

Let's face it – if Christianity is not true, then it would be crazy to follow Christ, but if it is true, then we should trust and follow Jesus, whether it gives us help or not and whatever other people may say. As a French novelist said, if fifty million people say a foolish thing, it is still a foolish thing.

And there's nothing foolish about trusting and following Jesus. People who do that enjoy a growing relationship with the Lord – as the apostle John put it, loving Him who first loved us (1 John 4:19).

Earlier I referred to Joni Eareckson who broke her neck in a diving accident. Later on, she looked back to the days when she could walk, run and ride a horse (she loved horses) and confessed that as a teenager she had been pretty self-centred.

She wrote: "I was trusting Christ as my Savior from sin, and I more or less tried to do what was right. But the basic thing on my mind when I thought about God was, 'What can He do for me? How can serving Christ give me joy? How do I feel at the end of a worship service?'" She refers to it as "a God-exists-to-make-me-happy mentality." She moved on from that, of course, as she grew in grace and the knowledge of Christ (2 Peter 3:18).

But, to return to our main question, we all need to consider where we stand, however we were brought up. If we were brought up to believe in God and go to church and so on, we need to consider for ourselves whether we really believe in the things we were brought up to believe, and if we were brought up without any religious influences at all, we need to consider for ourselves whether a non-religious attitude is the right one.

So how do we answer the idea that if we had been brought up in Iraq we might be Muslims. We have to admit that that's possible – but it doesn't change the basic question, which is: what is the truth about God? Is Islam or Hinduism or some other religion right, or is the Christian faith (which has been the foundation of western culture and of so many good things in our society) true?

Another answer to "You're only a Christian because that's the way you were brought up" is that with many people it simply isn't so. While there are some people who have turned their backs on the faith of their childhood, there are others who have come to believe in Jesus even though they had no Christian background. So there are no easy equations in this.

Could you excuse a wee bit shorter a letter this time. Granny wants me to go into town with her to do some shopping – what joy! But at least I've got a book token to spend. Thanks again for the present.

Grandad

13th June
Dear Sam,

What did you make of my last message
with thoughts on how to answer people
who say we're only Christians because
that's the way we were brought up? I suggested four things about
that idea:

    1. The same thing could be said about unbelievers – that they're
only unbelievers because that's the way *they* were brought up.

    2. It's true that upbringing is important and does affect us.

    3. Some people turn against the way they were brought up.

    4. And the big question is: which religion is true?

That last point reminds us that some people would say there
are many religions in the world and everybody should be left to
make their own choices, and no-one can say that one religion is
true and the others are false.

Well, it's a free country (or at least it used to be, before recent
times when there are certain things you're not supposed to even
think, never mind say. But that's another matter). People do need
to be left to make up their own minds where they stand and what
they believe.

But that doesn't mean that all religions are equally valuable or
equally true. When your dad was at school there was a Religious
Studies teacher who was explaining that pupils need to learn
about the different religions that exist in the world; she wrote,
"The main emphasis of any religious studies work is on the
promotion of tolerance. Everyone's viewpoint is valid."

The first part of that statement is fine – tolerance of others' views is a great thing – but what about the second part? Did that teacher really mean "Everyone's viewpoint is valid"? Does that include people who believe it's right to terrorise others, kill people or abuse children?

There's a story of a nature lesson in a class of seven-year-olds where a rabbit was brought in to the classroom. Some children thought it was a male rabbit; others that it was female. There was a lot of disagreement, and then one boy came up with what he thought was the solution – "Let's take a vote"! Well, obviously, taking a vote would make no difference – even if there was a unanimous vote for one option, that wouldn't affect the truth of the matter.

When it comes to religions, it just won't do to say, "Everyone's viewpoint is valid." For one thing, different religions say different things; they may agree on some points, but there are fundamental differences and if that's so they can't all be true.

Take people's view of Jesus. In some religions, Jesus is regarded as a good teacher or a prophet, but Christians believe that He is God's Son. That's a big difference and, just as we say that the two statements "the maximum speed on this road is 40 mph" and "the maximum speed on this road is 60 mph" can't both be true – so these opposing views of Jesus can't both be true, and we easily see that "everyone's viewpoint is valid" is not a valid statement.

Tolerance is a great virtue. We should treat people well and respect them even when we disagree about things. But nowadays the word is used in a different way. For many people, tolerance means accepting all beliefs as equal. That isn't what tolerance means. Tolerance means accepting that other people think

YOU'RE WEIRD

differently from the way you see things. You disagree with them, you are ready to discuss it with them and argue your case, but you still recognise that the other person has the right to decide for himself or herself.

And when it comes to "religious" matters, obviously we should respect people's freedom to follow their religion of choice, but that doesn't mean acting as if it doesn't matter what people believe, as if it were similar to whether you like pizza or not, which (no matter what your little brother thinks) is not a major life issue.

Unfortunately, history tells us that people have often done awful things to each other because of religious differences. It's terrible that it still happens and it ought not to be so.

But we shouldn't go to the extreme of saying that people's beliefs don't matter. Our basic beliefs determine a lot about our lives, our attitudes and our actions, and the Bible's challenge is to make up our minds to be (as an old hymn says) 'on the Lord's side'. We can respect others' right to believe or not, but for our own part we are called to follow One who actually said, "I am the truth" (John 14:6).

Near the end of his life, Moses said to the Hebrew people, "I have set before you life and death, blessing and curse" (Deuteronomy 30:19). The choice was theirs and Moses couldn't make that choice for them, but he went on to urge them, "Therefore choose life … loving the Lord your God, obeying his voice and holding fast to him."

There's a surprisingly strong message in Revelation 3:15 where Jesus said to the church in Laodicea, "Because you are lukewarm, and neither hot nor cold, I will spit you out of my mouth." That's vivid language; you don't expect to read in the Bible about people making Jesus sick, but that's what He was saying. Just as you want your drink to be either hot (if it's tea or coffee) or cold (if it's Coke or Pepsi) rather than lukewarm, so the Bible puts the choice before us and also urges us to choose life by trusting and obeying the Lord God.

Let me finish for today with an amusing thing I saw at the time of the last general election. You know how the authorities need to provide places where people can cast their vote (polling stations). Some schools are used and the pupils get the bonus of an extra holiday.

There was one school where there was a fence between the school and a busy road. Teachers must have been concerned about the possibility of pupils balancing on it, maybe with their lunchbox, so they put up a warning sign. And so on the election day there were two signs beside each other. One said, "Polling Station" and the other said, "Don't sit on the fence"!

"Sitting on the fence" is an expression we use when people can't make up their minds. The Bible challenges us: don't sit on the fence! In other words, make up your mind.

As Joshua said to the Israelites long ago, "Choose this day whom you will serve" (Joshua 24:15) before he went on to say, "As for me and my house, we will serve the Lord". And so, I hope, say all of us.

Love
Grandad

27th June
Dear Sam,

So Sean still says he's an atheist. Well, don't give up. As we've said before, nobody can argue someone else into the Kingdom of God. But one thing you can do is pray. I hope you pray for Sean and others like him. Pray what? Pray that the Holy Spirit will open his eyes to see the reality of Christ and His gospel. And pray that God will help you to be a good friend to Sean and a good witness too.

Talking about praying for the Holy Spirit to open his eyes reminds me of what Paul wrote in 2 Corinthians 4:4, "The god of this world has blinded the minds of the unbelievers, to keep them from seeing the light of the gospel of the glory of Christ, who is the image of God."

The same Paul reminds us elsewhere that the enemy is not the atheist but "spiritual forces of evil" (Ephesians 6:12). Paul went through the parts of a Roman soldier's equipment and likened each of them to different parts of the Christian's "armour" – the shield of faith, the sword of the Spirit, and so on, and at the end he urges us to keep praying.

In Paul's case he asked for prayer that "words may be given

me" (verse 19), and that's what I shall pray for you: that God would open your mouth and open Sean's ears.

You were saying that Sean talks about not needing God or religion. Many people today agree with him; they may say they don't object to religion, but they just don't feel any need of it. Others will suggest that Christianity is OK for little children who enjoy good stories (David and Goliath, and so on), or else they'll argue that it's actually wrong to introduce young children to its teachings before they have the ability to suss things out for themselves.

Mind you, all that really means is that *they*, unbelievers, should be free to teach young children their beliefs, namely that this world is all there is, that there isn't any God out there and that we don't need to bother with the Bible.

They don't think religion is important and they want to impart that idea to young children. So they say there should be no "religion" in schools. Of course, that means that there should be "secularism" in schools, but they don't think there's anything wrong with that. They leave aside the fact that our world really can't be understood without some knowledge of the Bible and of how Christianity has benefitted our society (we touched on that before – back in April, I think).

So, is it wrong to teach young children the truths of the Bible? Not at all. Parents and society have to make certain decisions for very young children even when they don't understand – in fact even when they object.

When you were very young, was there ever a day when you said, "Mummy, I think it's time you took me to the clinic to get a nurse to stick a sharp needle into my arm so that I don't get measles"? No, I didn't think so.

Did you decide it would be a good idea to go to school when you were five? I hope you'd agree now that it was a good idea – now that you know about the value of education – but back then you maybe were often pretty unwilling to go – you'd rather have stayed at home.

But such things are done for children for their own good, and the same applies to teaching them the message of the Bible.

Somebody else suggested to you that Christianity is just for old people, as if it's just meant to give some comfort in the thought of a life to come after they die. As a minister I've had to conduct many funeral services and I remember something said by an undertaker friend, who wasn't himself a Christian. He was thinking about all the "religious" aspects of funerals and said that if it did some good for mourners that was all that mattered. He didn't believe any of it, but he felt that if people are comforted by religious thoughts, that's OK; we just shouldn't think there's any reality in it.

It's the old idea that Christianity is a crutch. Everybody knows what a crutch is, and everybody wants to be able to walk and run without any crutches. They're for people who can't manage without them. And so, they say, Christianity is for people who can't manage, as others do, to cope with life as it is. Again it may sound like a strong argument, but is it really?

I once saw a Bible Society DVD about a boy who had cerebral palsy. He referred to this idea that Christianity is a crutch to lean on and went on to say that for him a crutch was essential and very helpful. If Christianity is a crutch, is that such a bad thing? I suppose it boils down to: is Christianity *just* a crutch?

The Bible's teaching is that all people are "handicapped" – in the sense that we are all sinners. People may not like the word "sin" but whether we like the word or not is hardly the point. And who could look around in this world and say they don't believe in sin? We hear about so many wrong things that people do, so much suffering that people cause to others.

But of course it's not just when we look around that we see the reality of sin; if we honestly look into our own hearts and lives, there too we know about the reality of sin. Who would deny it? Would any of us claim to be perfect – never telling lies or stealing or being envious?

And if it's true – that we are all sinners not only in our own eyes but before God who sees everything – then we need something to deal with that sin. We need to know that our sins can be forgiven.

And the message of Christianity is that when we admit our sin and sincerely confess it to God ("repent" is the Bible word for it), then He will forgive us and accept us (1 John 1:9). That's good news.

But back to that idea about Christianity being just a crutch: is it just that if you believe it and it helps you, then it's true for you? That's what many people will try to tell you – there's no such thing as truth; it's just a matter of "what's true for you".

But think about it – they're asking you to believe that there is no such thing as truth, except for the statement that there's no such thing as truth! They think that is true, even though they don't believe in truth.

But that's maybe enough for just now; it's time to give our brains a rest.

I hope everybody's fine there and we're looking forward to seeing you in the summer holidays.

Love
Grandad

14th July

Dear Sam,

OK, maybe we were getting a bit too intellectual last time. I know you're just a teenager, though I don't know about that word "just". And also I don't ever want to insult you by speaking to you as if you were still "just a child!"

We were thinking about the idea that Christianity is just a crutch, something to give you comfort when you need it and the pleasant thought that there's a "happy land" somewhere over the rainbow. It's the view that Christianity is just wishful thinking.

Remember how we thought once before about the idea that you only believe because of the way you were brought up – and how the very same thing could be said about many people who don't believe. The same applies here. The idea that Christianity is just wishful thinking can also be turned upside-down. What if unbelief and atheism are just wishful thinking?

One philosopher admitted that he wanted atheism to be true. He didn't like the fact that some of the most intelligent people he knew were (as he put it) religious believers, but he wrote: "It isn't just that I don't believe in God and, naturally, hope that I'm right in my belief. It's that I hope there is no God! I don't want there to be a God."

By the way, notice that he calls his atheism "my belief"; sometimes you'll hear an expression about people "of all faiths and none", but everybody believes some things. The atheist believes that God does not exist, that the universe came about by chance, that death is the end of our existence, and so on. Such notions are beliefs.

But anyway that philosopher said he didn't want there to be a God. At least that's honest. His faith is a kind of wishful-thinking faith.

Yet, many people will still claim that it's Christians who indulge in wishful thinking – hoping against hope that God is real and the Bible is true. They'll say, "You left behind belief in fairies and Father Christmas; however much you might wish they exist, they're not real. And isn't belief in God also something to leave behind as you grow up?"

The answer to that is that as Christians we're concerned not with what we'd like to be true but what is true.

Our faith is based on events that really happened in this real world. Everything about Christianity (the clue is in the name) centres in Jesus Christ. He was born at Bethlehem. There's so much mythology and sentimentality about Christmas that it would be easy to forget that the Baby was not just any old baby (or should that be any young baby).

When we were at your church last Christmas, we sang that Christmas song that says, "He came down to earth from heaven Who is God and Lord of all." This was God coming into this world, and the gospel is based on that coming and what He did when He died at Calvary.

There was a lady who wrote some hymns to help her godchildren to understand the phrases of what we call the Apostles' Creed. One of its phrases about Jesus is, "suffered under Pontius Pilate, was crucified, dead and buried", and the words she wrote on that subject are:

> We may not know, we cannot tell, what pains He had to bear,
> But we believe it was for us He hung and suffered there.
> He died that we might be forgiven, He died to make us good,
> That we might go at last to heaven,
> saved by His precious blood.

There's a story from the days of the Second World War when many British soldiers were captured by Japanese troops and often treated terribly. One squad had been working all day (slaving all day, as we would say) when a guard said that there was a shovel missing. He demanded to know who had taken it. Actually nobody had, but he ranted and raved at the men, saying that if no-one confessed, they would all be shot. As the guards raised their rifles, one prisoner stepped forward and said, "I did it."

The chief guard then started to beat him mercilessly, finally bringing the butt of his rifle down on the prisoner's head to smash his skull. Afterwards, when they got back to the prison camp, the tools were re-counted and it was found that there wasn't one missing after all.

So, why did that soldier say he had done it? To save the others. Are we going to criticise him for being untruthful? Not when he gave his own life so that the others might be spared.

That was amazing courage and self-sacrifice, and the Bible tells us that when Jesus died on the cross it wasn't because of any sins of His own. He took the blame for sin so that we might be saved. Not that we are innocent like these poor soldiers who hadn't stolen anything. In fact we're all guilty of wrong, but the gospel message is that God loved the world so much that He gave His Son so that whoever believes in Him should not perish but have eternal life (John 3:16).

And when the apostle Paul spoke about it, he used an interesting phrase. In Acts 26:26 he said to his questioners, "This thing was not done in a corner." What did he mean? He meant that Christianity is not about secret events known only to a few special people. It's all about real events in this real world.

It's not "too good to be true" and it's not wishful thinking.

And think about this as well: how can it be wishful thinking when many of the things we read in the Bible are not things we would wish at all? I'm thinking of the strong demands God makes on His people and even the strong words of Jesus.

For example, He talked about loving our friends but then went on, "But I say to you, Love your enemies" (Matthew 5:44). On another occasion He said, "If anyone would come after me, let him deny himself and take up his cross and follow me" (Mark 8:34).

If it were all wishful thinking, do you think we would have wished for that kind of thing? Hardly. Loving your enemy is difficult, and as for taking up your cross and following Jesus – well, when the first disciples heard that, they might have felt shivers down their spines, because everybody then knew what carrying a cross meant.

No, if it were a made-up story or just wishful thinking, the message would be very different from what it is.

Josh McDowell is a Christian evangelist and writer, but he has written about a time when "as a young man I set out to debunk Christianity... But then a funny thing happened. As I began investigating the claims of Christianity, I kept running up against the evidence."

In particular he studied the accounts in the four gospels of the resurrection of Jesus. "I had assumed that someone, or several someones, had invented the stories of Jesus Christ's resurrection from the dead. But as I examined these accounts, I had to face the fact that any sensible mythmaker would do things differently from the way Matthew, Mark, Luke and John did in recording the news of the Resurrection."

He went on to suggest a number of things that would be different if it were a made-up story. Here are some of them – and you'll see how different they are from what is recorded in Scripture:

• He would wait for a long time before publishing the story, so that people's memories had grown vague.

• Because of first century culture, he would never make women the first witnesses.

• He would have someone tell of actually seeing it (the resurrection) happening.

• He would portray the witnesses as heroes rather than people in fear of their lives.

• He would never suggest that some witnesses were still alive and you could go and ask them about it.

• He would stop short of dying for his beliefs.

• And he would imply that following Jesus is an easy option.

That last point is the point I was making. If the whole Christian message were wishful thinking, it wouldn't include the many warnings about how difficult it is to follow Jesus. Jesus said it demands self-denial instead of self-assertion and serving others instead of waiting for them to serve you. Christianity isn't for wimps.

Anyway, Sam, we're really looking forward to seeing you next week at Keswick. I'm glad your parents decided to take you there for part of the family holiday. You'll love it. Apart from the beauties of the Lake District, you'll enjoy the convention and the special groups for different age groups.

See you next week.

Grandad

31st July
Dear Sam,

Well, it wasn't quite up to Wimbledon standards, was it, but it was enjoyable – lawn tennis courts too! And how great was the rowing-boat on Derwentwater, even if we did sometimes seem to be going round in circles.

There was one of the convention meetings when the preacher spoke on the words of Romans 10:9 – "Jesus is Lord". I think you were at the youth meeting at the time and I don't know whether the theme was the same.

That phrase "Jesus is Lord" was introduced as one of the earliest Christian sound bites. And it certainly wouldn't square with the idea we considered last time about Christianity being wishful thinking. In the days after Jesus' death and resurrection it was a radical thing to believe and a much more radical thing to say out loud that Jesus was your Lord.

We're used to the word "Lord" so we sometimes miss its significance. When the Old Testament was translated from Hebrew into Greek, it's the word that was used to refer to Almighty God. The Old Testament name for Him was YHWH (usually pronounced Yah-way), a name that was regarded as so holy that ordinary people were unworthy to even say it.

So when the early Christians used the word to refer to Jesus, they were making a massive claim – staggering to the Jewish

people who had rejected Jesus. The disciples were saying that the man from Nazareth was God in the flesh.

Lord also means Master and when they called Jesus "Lord", that also meant that they wanted to follow His teaching and obey Him.

In the early days of Christianity this brought them into conflict with the Roman world where Caesar was regarded as Lord (sometimes God too). So when Paul wrote, "If you confess with your mouth that Jesus is Lord and believe in your heart that God raised him from the dead, you will be saved" (Romans 10:9) – that was asking a lot! It was not just a matter of believing certain things secretly in your heart – it was about saying openly that Jesus (yes, Jesus – not Caesar) is the Lord I will love and serve.

Calling Jesus your Lord was a bold step to take. And standing by that decision could sometimes be very costly. There was an elderly bishop called Polycarp, for example, who was told he must either blaspheme the name of Christ or die. Polycarp's often-quoted reply, before he was put to death, was, "Eighty-six years I have served him and he has done me no harm. How can I blaspheme my King who saved me?"

Much later in history there was a German pastor at the time when the Nazis were rising to power. Some members of the Hitlerjugend (Hitler youth) once threw a bomb into his manse. Why? It was because he had preached a sermon with the title, "Gott ist mein Fuhrer." I know you're studying Spanish and French but I think you'd know enough German to get that. He was saying "God is my leader, my Lord" – and that was dynamite, because it meant "God, not Hitler."

Maybe we're not likely to be put in such a situation, although we don't know what lies ahead. But still today it's a radical step to be openly known as a Christian. To use a big word, it's counter-cultural, which means going against the trend of society. It means saying Jesus – not money, pleasure, luck or even the state – is my Lord.

You've maybe seen in the papers the stories of some Christians who have been pressurised because of their faith. For example, there was a registrar who was unwilling to officiate at civil partnership ceremonies. The case went to court and during the case the government's lawyer argued that Christians must leave their faith at home or get another job!

Leaving your faith at home isn't really an option for people who follow Jesus. True, He said we shouldn't make a show of our religion before other people (Matthew 6:5), but it's also true that He calls us to "Stand up for Jesus" (do you know the hymn?). He said, "Let your light shine before others" (Matthew 5:16) and, "Whoever is ashamed of me and of my words in this adulterous and sinful generation, of him will the Son of Man be ashamed when he comes in the glory of his Father with the holy angels" (Mark 8:38).

At the end of the last chapter we saw that being a Christian often means going against the flow; discipleship isn't for wimps. If you seek to stand firm in your faith today, people may mock you and laugh at you. They may use words like stupid, out of touch, deluded, weird; for many people it's just not cool to follow Jesus seriously.

1 Peter 4:4 says that if you refuse to go along with wrong things others are doing, people will be surprised. He goes on to say that they forget one very important thing – one day we must all give account to God.

They also forget that God's instructions are given to enrich life and not to spoil it. Jesus said, "The thief comes only to steal and kill and destroy. I came that they may have life and have it abundantly" (John 10:10). The thief in that saying stands for anyone who tries to persuade people to abandon God's ways.

Before too long, you'll be thinking about learning to drive (better start saving up now). Part of the test involves reading the Highway Code. It's a few years since I passed the test (I think it was easier then) and my copy has a foreword by the person who was then the government's Minister of Transport – this is what it says about the Code:

"It deals with problems you will meet on the road, whether driving, walking or cycling. You may say, 'I don't need a book to tell me what to do'. But there are right and wrong ways of dealing with hazards and emergencies and even normal situations on the roads. If everyone always did things the right way we wouldn't have all the accidents we do. The Code explains the right way. The Code is not theory. It's a mine of practical, down-to-earth advice, it's a pocket life-saver. Please read it. Please do what it says."

You could read that again, substituting the Bible for the Code and it would reflect many of the claims that Christians make for God's Word. Next time I'll take up the question of why we should obey the Bible.

Love

Grandad

1st August
Dear Sam,

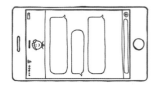

Why should we, in this modern world, follow the teaching of Someone who lived a long time ago in a world very different from ours? That's what many would say today: why should we go by what we read in the Bible?

There are several things that can be said about that:

• One is that the Bible is God's Word, not just a book of stories from long ago. 2 Peter 1:21 says, "No prophecy was ever produced by the will of man, but men spoke from God as they were carried along by the Holy Spirit." If God has said a thing, who are we to question or defy it?

• God's way is the best way. He made the world, He made us, and He knows the best way for us to live. Generally, it's a good idea to follow makers' instructions.

One of our cities has a motto, "Let Glasgow flourish by the preaching of the Word and the praising of His name." It is often shortened to "Let Glasgow flourish" – which just sounds like a wish for the material prosperity of the city, but the best kind of flourishing comes from heeding God's Word and praising His name.

• Another reason for following God's teaching in the Bible is the fact that we will all have to appear before God one day. Is that a frightening thought? It would be if we defy God's truth and reject his Son. As you know, Christianity isn't about trying to get good enough marks to get into heaven. Nobody would ever be saved that way. Salvation is not something to achieve but something to receive. As we read in Ephesians 2:8 – "By grace you have been saved through faith. And this is not your own doing; it is the gift of God, not a result of works." But then the next verse goes on to talk about the "good works, which God prepared beforehand, that we should walk in them."

• And that's the other answer to "Why should we heed God's book?" It's a matter of gratitude and love. Jesus said, "If you love me, you will keep my commandments" (John 14:15) and the apostle John drew it out: "By this we know that we have come to know him, if we keep his commandments." (1 John 2:3).

These are some reasons why we should pay heed to the Bible even in a society where many think that's daft.

And let's go on to think about some particular areas in which people are tempted to rebel against God's Word.

Take first Sunday, the Lord's Day. So many events nowadays are held on Sundays – sport, music, drama, whatever. And if you resolve to keep Sunday as the Lord's Day, people may try to argue you out of it and, if that doesn't work, call you stupid or old-fashioned. They may say that you'll never get ahead if you stick to that idea. Often it will be "just this once" – but we all know about that trap.

I suppose you know that the original commandment was about Saturday; that was and is the Jewish Sabbath. We call Sunday the Lord's Day because it was the day of Jesus' resurrection, and Christian people should certainly be in church unless something very serious prevents it. It is also meant to be a day of rest and my advice is to try to organise things so that you don't have to do homework or swot things up on Sunday.

Isaiah 58:13-14 says, "If you call the Sabbath a delight and the holy day of the Lord honourable, if you honour it, not going your own ways, or seeking your own pleasure, or talking idly, then you shall take delight in the Lord."

There have been many good examples of faithfulness in this matter, like the famous Eric Liddell. In more recent years the Scotland rugby player, Euan Murray, made the big decision that he would not play, even for his country, on a Sunday.

Another obvious pressure point concerns alcohol and drugs. You possibly know more about that scene than I do. Alcohol and drugs cause a lot of harm – in health, family problems, money problems, and so on. One NHS report said that a third of cases in Accident and Emergency Departments of hospitals are related to alcohol, and a recent survey in England showed that over half of police time is spent dealing with alcohol-related crimes.

We all have a responsibility to God to take care of the health He has given us (1 Corinthians 6:20), a responsibility to ourselves and a responsibility to other people (to set a good example). All in all, I hope you'll resist the pressure to just do what others are doing when it comes to alcohol and drugs. The temptation is to think, "Everybody else is doing it and I'll look like a freak if I don't" but really, people who try to persuade you to do things that are harmful to yourself and other people are not real friends.

The same goes for gambling, which is rife in our society from small-scale raffles to large-scale government-sponsored lotteries. It stands to reason that the dice are always going to be loaded in favour of the organisers; that's why gambling is sometimes called a mug's game. It has no place in the lives of people who seek to honour God and be responsible in our use of the gifts and resources He has given us.

Then there's language. That's another area in which Christians are challenged to be different from others. We're surrounded by swearing and blasphemy (the wrong use of the name of God or Jesus), and it may sometimes be tempting to think it cool to go along with it, but we need to make sure that we don't get into such a habit, and that our words are clean and loving.

And, of course, there's sex, but this e-mail is long enough already, so I'll write about that next time.

Grandad

15th August
Dear Sam,

In my last e-mail I wrote about some of
the ways in which "Jesus is Lord" applies
to our lives. Sometimes that means going
in a different direction from other people, in things like our
attitude to the Lord's Day and the use of the Lord's name.

Another area where Jesus is to be Lord is in sexual matters.
Years ago, few people actually spoke about sex, but now you can't
get away from it – in films, soaps and ordinary conversation.

And it's one of the main areas where modern society has
turned its back on God. The media are obsessed with it, and there
are many pressures to think that having sex with someone is not
that big a deal, even that it's up to you whether you link up with
someone of the same sex or the opposite sex.

In the next few years there are sure to be times of temptation
to think the same way as "everybody else" and even to just "do
what everybody else is doing". But, as you know, God's way is
that people should wait until they are married before they have
sex and that a husband and wife should then be faithful to each
other. There's no doubt about it – that's God's way.

Sometimes people think Christians are coy or embarrassed
to talk about sex, but when you think about it, a
Christian view starts from the fact that God thought
it up! He made us male and female and there's
nothing in the Bible to suggest that there's anything
sinful about sexual relationships. In fact the Bible
talks frankly about the joys of sex (for example,
Proverbs 5:19). But the big question is: why should

it be restricted to married couples? What's wrong with a bit of experimenting? Before I come to that, let me ask you to imagine

a train travelling along a railway track and saying, "These lines – they're so restrictive. Why should I have to stick to this track that somebody else laid long ago? Why shouldn't I be free to roam over the fields wherever I want to go?" Obviously the answer is that it's that restrictive track that enables a train to do what a train is meant to do and go where a train is meant to go.

The track isn't really restrictive. And God's commands aren't meant to spoil things but rather to enable people to be the best they can be. If the train were to go off the track, it would crash or get bogged down; just as when people reject God's way, it leads to trouble. I heard recently about a family where the husband has been unfaithful to his wife and the wife and children are heartbroken.

So why not just go along with "what everybody else is doing" (although it's worth remembering that some people talk big they're probably not actually doing it). Here are some things to think about on the subject:

First, sex is special and it *is* a big deal to be physically intimate with someone of the opposite sex. I said that sex was invented by God, and it's meant to be an enjoyable part of life with one's husband or wife. Sleeping around cheapens what is meant to be a very special thing. Treating it as a recreational activity (no strings attached) – even if you think you're going to spend the rest of your life with the person – doesn't provide a good basis for marriage.

If you eventually marry someone, it's not good to be comparing that person with others with whom you've been intimate.

In fact, we could make a simple equation: if you have sex with other people, you'll be left with regrets later – if you keep sex for marriage, you won't regret it.

Also, there are risks in early sexual activity, especially if you have sex with more than one person. Obviously there's the risk of pregnancy – even when contraception is used – and the birth of a baby ought to be a precious thing, not the unwanted result of casual sex. I expect you'll be told that condoms can usually prevent conception, but not always, and there's also the risk of sexually transmitted infections. You'll hear plenty of talk about "safe sex", but the only really safe sex is sex within a marriage between one man and one woman.

Some people talk casually about abortion – if a girl becomes pregnant, she can just "get rid of it", as if the "it" isn't a person. We need a better view of life than that – one that takes account of what the Bible says about God knowing us before we were born. It says, "You formed my inward parts; you knitted me together in my mother's womb" (Psalm 139:13-14). Life is a gift from God and it is to be respected and honoured.

Also, the early or promiscuous use of sex can lead to loads of pain and heartache. You may feel pressurised by "but everybody else is doing it" or you may hear people saying, "I'll probably lose my boyfriend or girlfriend if I don't" or even, "You're just chicken; I dare you". Some romantic friendships break up after a while – which is OK, but if there has been sexual activity, it can leave a lot of pain and awkwardness after the relationship ends.

There may come a time when you feel pressurised into living together (just moving in with someone), but statistics show (many people don't like to admit this) that couples who live together before being married have a fifty per cent greater risk of a marriage breakdown than those who don't.

Everything points to keeping sex for marriage. It's what Genesis says right from the beginning: "A man shall leave his father and mother and hold fast to his wife, and they shall become one flesh" (Genesis 2:24). That's the right order, and everything shows that it's the best way.

But of course it's not easy to go by the book and follow Christ in a sex-obsessed society. I really hope that you'll be persuaded in your mind that you're going to keep sex for marriage. And it's best to make up your mind about that before you have a one-to-one friendship with someone special.

Another important principle found in the Bible is that, if you're a Christian, you should ensure that the person with whom you become close shares your values and is also a Christian. The Bible has a lot to say about that, and I've seen it – someone who seemed to believe in Jesus then married an unbeliever and ended up without any living faith.

The main thing is – let your values be determined by God's Word. That will clash with what you hear elsewhere, including the sex-education class (or whatever they call it now) at school. You'll hear things that go against the Bible, and if there's a conflict between believing others (friends, teachers, pop stars, "celebrities" or anyone else) and believing God's Word, it's obvious which should come first.

By the way, you do have a helpful resource in people called parents. You may think they wouldn't understand, but actually your parents were once your age, and they only want to help you be the best you can be. If you can keep open lines of communication with your parents and discuss all sorts of things with them, that will be good.

A good text to finish with is Romans 12:2 – "Do not be conformed to this world, but be transformed by the renewal of your mind that by testing you may discern what is the will of God, what is good and acceptable and perfect." That's the way to go.

Love from Granny and Grandad

22nd August
Dear Sam,

No, I don't mind you asking about
homosexual relationships. Maybe I
should have gone on to that last week but I thought the letter was
long enough without starting on a new subject.

You'll find this hard to believe, but when I was a boy the word
"gay" meant happy or cheerful. I don't know how the word came
to be used for homosexual people. But you've been wondering
what's the Christian attitude on this subject that is put right
before us these days.

The pressure to conform to the ways of the world is strong,
and it's very unpopular to disagree with the world's ways. I
expect you've heard many people (even "officially") tell you that
homosexual relationships (boy/boy or girl/girl) are OK, and
if you even raise an eyebrow, you'll be called an intolerant and
homophobic bigot. Our governments have even authorised the
non-sense of same-sex "marriage".

Probably we should start from the fact – and it's often
overlooked – that many teenagers experience a stage
in their development when they are attracted
to someone of the same sex – someone they
admire and want to be like. That's a normal
part of growing up and it has nothing to
do with being a homosexual.

But some people find, even
when they're older, that they are
still attracted to people of the same
sex. I can't imagine what that must

be like, especially for Christians who know that the Bible says homosexual practice is wrong and displeasing to God. They know that they can't help how they feel, but as Christians they can't act on the basis of these feelings. In fact that means they live their lives like all the single people who are Christians.

Of course there's no justification for bigotry or "gay-bashing." It's wrong to look down on people or make fun of them for any reason. For one thing, it's not for us to condemn others – not when Jesus said He didn't come to condemn the world but that the world might be saved (John 3:17).

We see that in action in the story of the woman who was dragged before Him because she'd been found in bed with a man who wasn't her husband. Some people expected Jesus to

condemn her, but remember how he sat doodling in the sand. Then He challenged anyone who was sinless to speak up, and to the woman He said, "I do not condemn you; go, and from now on sin no more" (John 8:3-11).

He didn't deny that she had sinned (by the way, why didn't they bring the man to Jesus as well?), but He told her to change her ways.

That's Jesus' way, and of course the whole Bible encourages us to love other people, whoever they are and whatever they have done. You'll find that in passages like: Leviticus 19:17-18, Matthew 22:37-39, Romans 13:9-10, 1 Corinthians 13:4-5 and 1 Corinthians 16:14. We are to love, value and respect other people. The important thing is that we shouldn't form our views from the standards of the world but from the Word of the Lord.

A Member of Parliament once said about the Church of England that if it wanted to be a national church it would have to reflect the values of the nation. According to the Bible, the church isn't at liberty to do that. We are not to follow the world's agenda. The church's first responsibility is to be true to its Master and what He has caused to be written down.

I remember you once went to see *Jungle Book*; well the book was written by Rudyard Kipling, who wrote somewhere about a village where people were arguing about whether the world is round or flat. Eventually they took a vote and the majority decision was that the earth is flat! Did that change anything? Obviously not – the earth is a sphere and that's all there is to it.

And we are not asked to vote on whether God's teaching is right or not.

There are two big questions about this (or any) subject: "What does the Bible say about it?" and "Why does that matter?"

As to the first, the Bible doesn't speak about people being attracted to others of the same sex, but it does say that homosexual practice is sinful. If you want to check that out, you could look up: Genesis 1:17 and 2:24, Leviticus 18:22, Matthew 19:4-5, Romans 1:21-27, 1 Corinthians 6:9-11.

But the other question is: why should twenty-first century people be bound by words written down long ago? The answer is: because it is God's Word. As 2 Timothy 3:16 says, "All Scripture is breathed out by God".

We should also say that if Christianity is about trusting and following Jesus, then that means following Him in what He says about the Bible as well as everything else, and in John 10:35 he said plainly, "Scripture cannot be broken."

About the New Testament, He said to His disciples, "These things I have spoken to you while I am still with you. But the Holy Spirit will teach you all things and bring to your remembrance all that I have said to you." (John 14:25-26) Jesus' plan was that these disciples would be guided to write God's Word down for the instruction and guidance of all of us who would come after.

Jesus once praised John the Baptist because he wasn't like "a reed shaken by the wind" (Matthew 11:7). A reed just bends with whatever way the wind is blowing. But John set the example of standing firm. And, as we've said, this is one area where, more than any other, you'll be under pressure to bend with the wind, but God calls us first and foremost to obey Him and His Word.

Another thing to mention is that you need to be careful about the magazines and books you read and the films you watch. It's especially true about the internet. There's a lot of wicked stuff out there, and some of your friends may look at it, but that doesn't mean you have to do the same.

Martin Luther had an amusing way of putting it: he said you can't help birds flying over your head, but you can prevent them building their nests in your hair.

As I said in my last letter, God's way is that sexual relationships are to be enjoyed (which is important to remember, by the way)

between a man and a woman committed to each other in marriage. Anything else is – we might as well say it plainly – wrong.

The Bible tells us about one young guy who was tempted to have sex with a woman who wasn't his wife. It was Joseph. He worked in a grand house, and his employer's wife started making advances toward him. He kept refusing to do wrong, and eventually had to literally run away. You can read the story in Genesis 39, and it reminds us that "fleeing from sexual immorality" (1 Corinthians 6:18) is not a sign of weakness or wimpishness but of self-control, strength and maturity.

In all of these areas, following Jesus will make you different from many people, and it may be tempting sometimes to wish you could just be like them. Peer pressure is a strong thing, but God's call is for people who will not just follow the crowd and conform to the world's standards but who will allow God to shape them in His way.

It's Romans 12:2 again — which was paraphrased by J. B. Phillips: "Don't let the world around you squeeze you into its own mould, but let God re-mould your minds from within, so that you may prove in practice that the plan of God for you is good."

Love

Grandad

P.S. Granny and I will be on holiday for a few weeks, so maybe it'll be longer than usual till my next letter. But, always glad to hear from you …

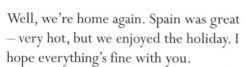
18th September
Dear Sam,

Well, we're home again. Spain was great
– very hot, but we enjoyed the holiday. I
hope everything's fine with you.

Recently we've been thinking about things that turn people
off Christianity, and another that we mentioned earlier is the
church! That's ironic, of course, because the church is meant
to help people to believe, but nowadays some people will think
you're a bit of an odd-bod if you go to church or belong to any
Christian organisation. For many people in the U.K. church is
good for Christmas Eve, a funeral or the occasional wedding, but
that's about all.

What is it about the church's life that puts people off? Part of
it is the church's history, and I'm afraid we can't deny that grim
things have been done in the name of Christianity. Others will
refer to someone they know (or know about) who's "supposed to
be a Christian" but doesn't live up to the ideals of the Bible.

Unfortunately, we've all heard news stories about abusive
priests or some minister or bishop who has been in the headlines
for all the wrong reasons. The media love it when they can find a
Christian leader who has left the straight and narrow or says he
doesn't believe or preach the basic truths of Christianity.

Then there are the various divisions and
splits that have happened within the church –
things that lead some people to say, "If Christians
can't even agree with each other, why should we
want to be part of their church?"

And, of course, others will say that going to

church is dull and boring or that it's just for old folk. They can't see why they should give up some of their precious time to sit on hard seats in a building that is bound to be either too cold or too hot and listen to some guy going on and on about things from an old book.

And yet another thing we sometimes hear is, "You can live a good life, or even be a Christian, without going to church?"

I wrote about the first issue (the church's history) back in April, so let me turn here to some of these other things we've mentioned.

What on earth can we say to people who've been put off by someone who's "supposed to be a Christian", but their life doesn't square with it? I heard of a minister who asked members of his church to suggest reasons why Christianity was unpopular among the people they worked with. Lots of reasons were given, but the most frequent was something like, "Christianity's OK; it's Christians who are a pain in the neck"!

So, what can we say? We can start with the fact that the church is made up of ordinary human beings – sinners – who admit that they aren't what they should be. Nobody fully lives up to the teaching of Jesus. His standard is so high – not the standard for

becoming a Christian. In one way, that's simple – it's a matter of asking God to forgive your sins in Jesus' name and asking Him into your life as your Saviour and Lord.

But once you've done that, you are called to follow Him and His teaching – and the standard is set high. It's not just about never doing anyone any harm (that's what many people imagine). It's not just about giving up your seat in the bus to an old lady and giving a donation to Oxfam every so often. Of course it's good to be kind to old

ladies and to give to charity, but there's more to
Christian living than that.

One of the striking things about Jesus'
teaching is that He was strongly against
hypocrisy. The word means acting a part, and
Christ has no time for a purely outward show of
religion.

On one occasion, He even likened some
people to "whitewashed tombs, which look fine
on the outside but are full of bones and decaying
corpses on the inside. In the same way, on the outside you appear
good to everybody, but inside you are full of hypocrisy and sins."
(Matthew 23:27-28 in the Good News Bible) Saying that sort
of thing wasn't going to make Him popular with everybody, but
He didn't tone down His teaching in order to please people or
attract followers.

So we have to simply agree that Christians are imperfect – but
also suggest that accusing Christians of being pure hypocrites
is unfair to many people who, for all their faults, are trying to
follow Jesus.

The difference between a hypocrite and such a Christian
who is trying to follow Jesus comes out in one of His stories,
a story which we're told was directed at "some who trusted in
themselves that they were righteous, and treated others with
contempt."

It's a story about two men who went to church to pray. One
of them was proud of his own goodness and prayed, "God, I
thank you that I am not like other men, extortioners, unjust,
adulterers, or even like this tax collector. I fast twice a week; I
give tithes of all that I get." The other guy wouldn't even lift his
eyes to heaven but simply prayed, "God, be merciful to me, a
sinner!" (Luke 12:9-14)

Now, you don't need to be a Doctor of Theology to know which one Jesus commended, do you? The second admitted his sin and prayed for mercy.

And if people come to receive that mercy and grace, they are called to follow Jesus day by day, asking for the Holy Spirit's strength to become more like Jesus.

People may point to the faults and failings of Christians, but that's no reason to reject Christianity.

You know these catalogues that come through the letter-box (we get about four a week); I remember seeing one that had an advert for a secure container where you could keep your money and valuables. It looked like a tin of beans, and the idea was that a burglar would hardly think that your most precious things were stored in a bean tin. Paul had another way of putting it: "We have this treasure in jars of clay" (2 Corinthians 4:7).

The message for people who attack the failings of Christians is: don't judge Christianity by the lives of its worst examples; in fact don't judge it by any of its examples. Don't concentrate on the clay jars but on the treasure.

And the treasure is Jesus. He is the One to trust and follow. When we invite others to become Christians, we aren't inviting them to trust and follow us but to trust and follow Him. Christianity, after all, is all about Jesus.

There are some things to think about. More next time.

*Love
Grandad*

3rd October
Dear Sam,

You're quite right. I only went so far
in trying to give you answers about the
church. I hope what I wrote about the accusation of hypocrisy
was helpful, but what about some of the other criticisms that are
made against the church.

First of all, what can we say to people who criticise the
divisions and splits within the church and say, "If Christians can't
even agree with each other, why should we have anything to do
with their Christianity?"

One reply is that, even if Christians disagree about some
things, they would still regard the message they share as much
more important. In churches like yours, for example, babies
are baptised, while other churches only baptise adult believers.
People can differ about that while agreeing on the main things
about Jesus being the Saviour of those who trust Him.

It's like people disagreeing about which football team to
support but still agreeing (as I know you would) that football is
a great game. Christians should strive for unity, but the church's
divisions don't really discredit Christianity.

There's also the fact that we are talking about things of the
greatest importance – so maybe it's not surprising that people
should see some things differently. It's not like a hobby (say, chess
or minecraft) – where not much is at stake. People's attitude to
Jesus is all-important, both for this life and for the life to come.

And think of this: would anyone look at a building site and
complain about all the mess – heaps of bricks, piles of timber, JCBs
and other vehicles cluttering the place. Would anyone say, "Doesn't

look much like a house to me"? If anyone did, the answer would be, "But the job isn't finished yet; when the work is completed, everything will be tidied up and there will be a fine new building."

Well, the church is, in a way, God's building site. There's a song:

God is building a house, God is building a house,
God is building a house that will stand.
He is building by His plan with the living stones of man;
God is building a house that will stand.

One day it will be completed, and the invitation of the gospel is to be part of this great work that God is doing. In one of the passages I mentioned before, Paul wrote down a list of some sins that people commit, and then he wrote, "And such were some of you" (1 Corinthians 6:11). Think about that word "were"? It speaks of what they used to be – but Jesus was changing them day by day.

You also told me about some of your pals who say church is boring. It reminded me of one entertainer who described church services as "The dullest experience we have in this country"! Is it just that he had a particularly bad experience? Or is he right?

Well, it can be – boring, that is. People who attend services often do so out of pure habit and it isn't unknown for people to be counting the number of panes in stained-glass windows or doing mental arithmetic with the numbers on the hymn board. I've attended some services where the singing is dire, the prayers are soooo loooong and the sermon seems to go on forever!

But the New Testament describes a church that certainly wasn't boring. There was a vitality and joy that proved attractive to outsiders.

There's a little description of that early church at the end of

Acts 2 where we're told that the Christians devoted themselves to four things:

1. To the apostles' teaching, which they had received from Jesus Himself. It's what is now written in Scripture.

2. To the fellowship. There was a great sense of togetherness. Whatever their differences they had a shared faith in Jesus that drew them together.

3. To the breaking of bread. That's what we usually call communion (or, in some churches, the eucharist).

4. And to prayer. That's pretty central to Christianity – with the confidence that God hears your prayers, whether on your own or in a group.

The last verse of the chapter talks about them "praising God and having favour with all the people. And the Lord added to their number day by day those who were being saved." There was a vitality and excitement about the life of the church and it spilled over into the world.

Of course, it wasn't that everybody loved them. There were enemies of the gospel, and before very long fierce persecution broke out against Christianity and Christians (thrown to the lions, etc).

But why the excitement? It was because of the good news that is at the heart of the church's life. That good news is explained in the apostles' teaching, enjoyed in company with others, shared in communion and expressed in prayer.

It's about God dealing with the fundamental flaw in human experience which messes up life in this world. It's about a salvation that affects the past – because it deals with sin and guilt; it affects the future – because it's about the promise of eternal life with Christ; and it affects the present – because it gives a sense of purpose

and direction to life and assures us of the Holy Spirit's help in our efforts to become more Christ-like.

People who appreciate these truths will surely be excited about the gospel and eager to share in worship. There have been people who once found church boring, but then something happened (they would say they were converted or God opened their eyes) and the same services became very un-boring. They were able to enter into the worship and wanted to learn more from God's Word. Sometimes people have found it so thrilling that they can't understand why everyone else in the world doesn't see it the way they do.

That's one thing about the notion that church is boring. It shouldn't be.

We can also say: thank God, it isn't like that everywhere. I suppose we have to admit that some churches do seem to have boredom written in to their constitutions, but sometimes when people say "church is boring", they're just remembering a few bad experiences; it might even be worth asking when they last actually attended a service.

I remember a Premier League football match I attended where the game was an absolute bore. One of the ball-boys was doing tricks with the ball about behind the goal and that proved more entertaining than the game! But if I drew the conclusion, "Football is boring", someone would say to me, "Don't judge the sport by one poor match."

And people shouldn't judge the church by a few memories of bad experiences. Many churches have changed a lot and often there is a liveliness and sense of joy, as I know there is in your church. I suppose if people go along determined to be bored, they will be bored; far better to approach church with the desire to find out more about the message of Christ and to express thanksgiving and worship to Him. Also, your presence can be a great encouragement to others.

That leaves one other thing which I'll come back to, but I hope you have great services tomorrow, and every Sunday, and that you can help others to see that it shouldn't be boring, it isn't always boring and it needn't be boring.

Grandad

16th October
Dear Sam,

I was glad to get your e-mail last week about your own experience of church and I was happy to hear that you "enjoy" going. Of course we don't go to church to be entertained, but I know what you mean. It's great when people feel on Sunday morning, "Oh good – church today."

I hope that you do succeed in getting some of your friends to go too. There's a liveliness about your church and people coming in as newcomers or visitors (like us) find it relaxed and welcoming. There may sometimes be a song or psalm you don't know, or one that seems a bit old-fashioned, but there are also many new songs and contemporary hymns. And it's great that you have a minister who works hard on his sermons to explain what the Bible passage means and how it applies to us today.

But the thing I left hanging over from last time is: "You can live a good life and be a good Christian without going to church". That's what many people would say, and what do we say about it?

 Can you be a Christian without attending church? Well, remember first that some Christians simply can't attend church. It may be because of illness or infirmity or because they live in parts of the world where either there is no church or the authorities threaten people who go to church with persecution and even death. Nobody would say that such people can't be Christians because they can't attend church. They can still trust in God, love Him and pray to Him.

But normally Christian commitment involves being part of the life of the church and the Bible spells that out in Hebrews 10:25 where we're told not to neglect meeting together. Actually it adds, "As some do" – which maybe tells us that even then some people were saying you didn't need to go to church to be a Christian. But according to the Bible, we jolly well should be in church unless something serious prevents it.

Christians are called to support one another. In *X-Men: Legacy* there's a character who says, "Ah know ah been talkin' a lot about standin' on your own. And that's good. We all gotta do that. But it's a lot easier to stand alone when you have friends to help you do it"!

That's true about discipleship too. Christian fellowship is a great advantage. Young and old, male and female, can value each other, and neither nationality nor social divisions are a barrier to fellowship. It's what led Paul to say to the people in the early church, "There is neither Jew nor Greek, there is neither slave nor free, there is no male and female for you are all one in Christ Jesus." (Galatians 3:28). He didn't mean that these distinctions no longer exist but that they don't matter within Christian fellowship.

You could say that the church is a bit like a band or orchestra where the instruments are very different from each other (guitar, trombone, keyboard, etc), but they work together to produce one piece of music as they follow one conductor or leader. You can think it out and consider how that picture fits the church.

Psalm 133:1 says, "How good and pleasant it is when brothers dwell in unity." And there's another Psalm which says, "I was glad when they said to me, 'Let us go to the house of the Lord!'" (Psalm 122:1) If you really appreciate the message of the gospel, then it will be a joy to share with other believers in worship.

And we do need it. Just as you can't play rugby or hockey on your own – you need to be part of a team – so it is that we need to be part of a living church if we are going to grow as Christians.

I wouldn't be surprised if your minister has told the story about somebody saying he didn't need to go to church to live a Christian life. The conversation took place beside a real fire (with coal and wood!) and the other person lifted the tongs, took one of the coals from the fire and placed it on the hearth. They watched as it burned, then smoked, then fizzled out. The point was made.

If we are seeking to live Christian lives in this world, we need every help we can get, and belonging to a church is part of that help. People say there's strength in numbers and there is certainly strength in Christian fellowship. It is within the church that we have the opportunity to learn from one another and support one another. How?

• Well, you can pray and worship on your own – of course you can, and should – but there's something special about joining with others. Being part of the worshipping community helps us all, and it's a two-way process with young and old being an encouragement to each other. Maybe the singing isn't of epic quality but it's the corporate praise of the local church and also part of the worldwide praise of the whole church.

• It's in church that we have the opportunity to learn together from God's Word, both in the Sunday services and in any small groups that you can join. Again, you can read the Bible on your own – and of course you should – but there's something special about learning together. Your minister spends a lot of time during the

week studying the Bible and preparing to open it up in a relevant way. And in other groups, the young can learn from the old and the old can learn from the young.

• Acting together is another great advantage. Being part of the church helps in caring ventures and in outreach. We sometimes feel that we can't accomplish much on our own (which is untrue actually) but we can accomplish more when we act together in Christian service and evangelism. All Christians are called to stand up for Jesus individually (like Daniel) but also corporately. Nobody would say that it's easy to evangelise today but it can be more effective when we act together

So we've been thinking about people saying "I can be a good Christian without going to church". There are also people who say things like, "You can live a good life without being a Christian." That's true, and we should always be glad to hear about deeds of love and kindness, whoever performs them.

It's also true, however, that the best of people fall short of being all that human beings should be. Few people would argue with Romans 3:23 that says, "All have sinned and fall short of the glory of God."

In fact, it's interesting to notice what Paul wrote about himself. Sometimes he introduced himself as "an apostle of Christ Jesus", but he could also write, "Wretched man that I am" (Romans 3:24). He wasn't glorying in his own imperfections and sins, but he was openly admitting that he wasn't all he should be. And then, later (towards the end of his life in this world) he wrote, "Christ Jesus came into the world to save sinners, of whom I am the foremost" (1 Timothy 1:15).

God doesn't want to rub our noses in our failures and sins; He wants people to come to Him and receive His forgiveness and salvation and then make progress as disciples and followers of Jesus.

There's an interesting testimony from John Newton who

wrote one of the most popular hymns ever written (*Amazing Grace*). He also wrote:

> I am not what I ought to be;
> I am not what I wish to be;
> I am not what I hope to be;
> but I am not what I was
> and by the grace of God
> I am what I am.

So, can you be a good person without being a Christian, and can you be a Christian without being part of the church? Yes and no! Non-Christian people do good and some Christians are (as we've seen) unable to attend church for one reason or another – although they are still part of the church even though they can't attend the services.

But much depends on definitions, both of Christian and church. A Christian is not just someone who tries his or her best to please God, but someone who admits to being a sinner and trusts in Christ as a loving Saviour and Lord.

And the church is not just a club for people who enjoy the same pursuits, like a judo club or trekkies group. It's the fellowship of those who are trusting in Christ and seeking to follow Him. Within that fellowship we support and help one another along the way, and there can't be anything boring about that!

I hope that this has given you some ideas about how to answer these things people say; also, that your church will help you in your Christian life and that you'll be a blessing to others.

Grandad

1st November
Dear Sam,

Sorry I've fallen behind in replying to
your message – but better late than
never. When I wrote last time we were
just about to start our church's autumn holiday club.

We had millions of children – at least it sounded like that.
But once again we found (I'm sure you've noticed) that it's fairly
easy to get little children to come but much more difficult with
your age-group. We had a café-style outreach in the evenings,
and some of the kids who came raised a few of the very questions
we've been thinking about – things like, "How can you believe
in God when there's so much suffering in the world?", "People
are only Christians because that's the way they were brought up"
and so on. I hope if you'd been here you would have been able to
answer some of the questions they were asking.

I suppose one of the biggest obstacles to the spreading of the
Christian faith is the feeling of many people that they just don't
need God or religion. They'd rather concentrate on becoming as
rich and successful as possible, as if that's what matters most in
life. Sometimes people just think such a thing without saying it out
loud. Or they'll say – and I guess many of your contemporaries
would say it – enjoying yourself is the main thing in life.

One of Jesus' stories is about that. A rich farmer concentrated
all his energy on getting richer and richer with the hope that one
day he'd be able to say to himself, "You have ample goods laid up
for many years; relax, eat, drink and be merry". (Luke 12:15-21)

But God said to the man, "Fool! This night your soul is
required of you, and the things you have prepared, whose will

they be?". That farmer forgot that we are all going to appear before God one day, and then it won't matter whether we were rich or poor. Jesus finished the parable with, "So is the one who lays up treasure for himself and is not rich towards God".

Of course Jesus wasn't saying there's anything wrong with being rich (or with being a farmer! – added in case your uncle Alex sees this message). The man's mistake was that he forgot that there are more important things in life than money and success. In fact, Jesus introduced the story with: "Take care, and be on your guard against all covetousness, for one's life does not consist in the abundance of one's possessions".

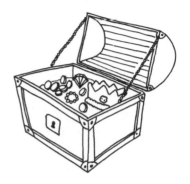

Once there was a preacher who said he was going to preach on this theme. He gave his message a rather long title: "YOU MUST NOT THINK YOU ARE IN THIS WORLD TO MAKE MONEY". That's something you might expect a preacher to say, but the person who was noting it for the service-sheet got the punctuation wrong, and put a full-stop after the word "THINK". It read, "YOU MUST NOT THINK. YOU ARE IN THIS WORLD TO MAKE MONEY". It's just a little dot, but what a difference!

And what folly to pursue either of these statements when they're separated like that. We shouldn't think we are in this world to make as much money as possible; that's not the main thing in life.

Of course it's good to do well in schoolwork and exams so that you have good prospects – satisfying job, good wages or salary, decent standard of living. There's nothing wrong with that, but it's like the farmer in the parable: it wasn't foolish to become rich but it was foolish to ignore the more important things in life. Jesus said he was foolish to concentrate on laying up treasure for himself without being rich towards God.

Many people have spoken about becoming rich (materially and financially) and still not being satisfied – like a once-famous actor who spoke about sitting on top of the world, having wealth and fame: "I could have anything money could buy. Yet I found that at the top of the world there was nothing."

In Old Testament times, Solomon was probably one of the richest men in the world, but consider this that he wrote in Ecclesiastes 2:

"I made great works. I built houses and planted vineyards for myself. I made myself gardens and parks, and planted in them all kinds of fruit trees. I made myself pools from which to water the forest of growing trees. I bought male and female slaves, and had slaves who were born in my house. I had also great possessions of herds and flocks, more than any who had been before me in Jerusalem. I also gathered for myself silver and gold and the treasure of kings and provinces..."

That may sound like success, but his conclusion was, "He who loves money will not be satisfied with money, nor he who loves wealth with his income; this is vanity." That whole book of the Bible (Ecclesiastes) shows up the futility of a life without God. We are made for a relationship with Him and without Him life will always be incomplete.

In the New Testament, Paul reminded his young friend Timothy, "We brought nothing into this world, and we cannot take anything out of the world" (1 Timothy 6:7). He went on to say that those who desire to be rich – who make that their main aim in life – "fall into temptation, into a snare, into many senseless and harmful desires that plunge people into ruin and destruction."

He also tells those who are rich not to be haughty, nor to set their hopes on the uncertainty of riches, but on God, who richly provides us with everything to enjoy (verse 17).

Somebody once sent me one of these e-mails that go round with jokes or puzzles. It was a riddle and the e-mail said that seventy per cent of primary school children solved it, but only seventeen per cent of university students could figure it out. Here's the riddle:

It's more powerful than God.

It's more evil than the devil.

The poor have it.

The rich need it.

If you eat it you will die.

Any ideas? The e-mail was one of those where you have to scroll down to get the answer, and what is it that most primary school pupils but only seventeen per cent of university students could solve?

I'll come to the answer in a moment, but first consider another puzzle: take Jesus' words in Matthew 6:24, and imagine that something had happened to the manuscript and the last word was missing so that it read, "You cannot serve God and …".

If you were asked to guess what the next word must have been, what would you think? Would it be "You cannot serve God and the devil" or "God and sin" or "God and yourself"? How many people would have guessed that the last word is "money"? That's what He said: "You cannot serve God and money." It's interesting that He didn't say, "You cannot *have* God and money" – it's all about what matters most to us.

And the answer to the first puzzle? It's nothing!

Nothing is more powerful than God.

Nothing is more evil than the devil.

The poor have nothing.

The rich need nothing.

If you eat nothing you will die.

But wait a minute; that fourth line – is it true? Perhaps people can become so rich that they don't need any thing, but it isn't true to say that the rich need nothing. Everyone needs things that money can't buy – things like an answer to our guilt about doing wrong and an answer to our anxiety about the future. Such things are found not in possessions but through faith in Jesus. And the invitation is for everyone, rich or poor.

Anyway, I'll stop for now and hope there won't be such a gap before the next time.

Love

Grandad

20th November
Dear Sam,

Don't the days go by quickly at this
time of year? Shops seem to start earlier
every year with their Christmas displays, but it's a bit early to be
hearing Jingle Bells or even Silent Night.

However, I believe you have the small matter of class tests
before you can think about Christmas, and I hope you get on
well. You'll need your thinking cap on.

Talking about thinking caps, I heard someone
saying sarcastically that when people go to church
they need to hang up their brains at the door
with their coat and hat. I'm sure you'd never
think such a thing; we know that God's call is to
love Him with all of our mind as well as all of our
soul, strength and heart (Mark 12:30).

We know, don't we, that nobody is ever saved
through intellect. I've always loved the saying of a
Dutch theologian called Erasmus. He referred to
the criminal crucified beside Jesus, the one who said, "Remember
me when you come into your kingdom." (Luke 23:42) Jesus
replied, "Today you will be with me in Paradise". Well, Erasmus
said that that so-called penitent thief was his favourite Bible
character because he was "saved with so little theology"!

But it's also true that we are to use whatever brain-power God
has given us in our discipleship and service.

It's either a silly mistake or a snide attack to say, as some
people do, that Christianity is just for simple, uneducated or
unthinking people who are gullible enough to believe it all.

You know the kind of thing: "Nobody can believe nowadays that somebody could walk on water or survive after being swallowed by a whale".

I'll leave miracles till next time, but for the moment, we can be thankful that the gospel is for people at all levels of intellect.

I remember referring earlier to a philosopher who said he wanted atheism to be true. He also said that he was disturbed by the fact that some of the most intelligent and well-informed people he knew were religious believers.

One writer (in a book called *How To Give Away Your Faith*) wrote about people saying, "If Christianity is true, why do so many intelligent people not believe it?" Then he went on, "The answer is precisely the same as the reason why so many unintelligent people don't believe. They don't want to because they're unwilling to accept the moral demands it would make on their lives."

Is that too hard? Sometimes people do have genuine questions

about faith and the Bible, and I hope that our discussions over this past year have helped you to give a reasonable answer to some of the things people say. But sometimes people simply don't want to believe because of what that might mean for them.

You've had the advantage of being taught from your earliest days to believe, like Timothy in the New Testament who knew from childhood the message that can "make you wise for salvation through faith in Christ Jesus." (2 Timothy 3:15)

But, as you know very well, it's not easy to go on in Christian discipleship. I guess you'd recognise what I'm talking about when I refer to the temptation to hide your faith in certain company – like the chameleon that can change its colour to fit in with its surroundings. Many people are tempted to do that — be faithful when they're with Christian friends but at other times keep their faith hidden.

There's an interesting story about some graffiti found in Rome in the nineteenth century. Scholars date it in the second or third century. It's a drawing of a man on a cross but with a donkey's head, and the caption beside it says, "Alexamenos worships his God".

Alexamenos was possibly a young Roman soldier who was (as one hymn says) "not ashamed to own his Lord". Maybe the other soldiers mocked him and taunted him. But he stuck to his guns. And in the next room there was another message — in Latin, "Alexamenos fidelis" (is faithful).

He wasn't like a chameleon; he was faithful to Christ through thick and thin.

He was probably young and it's interesting to remember that many of the most important decisions you make are made when you're young. It's usually when you're young that you choose a job or career; many people fall in love with "that special person" while they're young — a bit older than you, I hope, but you know what I'm talking about (just think of your madly-in-love sister). Your political views may be formed when you're young, along with much that affects the direction of your life.

The famous atheist Lord Russell wrote, "My character, tastes and ideals were, in the main, fixed by the time I reached the age of sixteen." Of course people can change later in life, but it's still true that many important things are decided when you're young.

And the most important thing of all is responding to the call of Jesus to set out on His way. Hebrews 12:1-2 likens it to a race: "Let us lay aside every weight, and sin which clings so closely, and let

us run with patience the race that is set before us, looking to Jesus".

If we think of it as a race, it's more like a marathon than a sprint. It's a bit like the steeplechase because sometimes there are hurdles. And we might also think of it as a relay race; others have passed the baton on to us and it is for us to pass it on to others.

A famous evangelist once said that at one of his meetings 17½ people were converted. Was that seventeen adults and one child? No, he explained, he meant the opposite: seventeen young people who had their whole lives stretching out before them and one adult whose life was already halfway through. It's a wonderful thing to trust and follow Jesus from early in your life and to give Him your whole life.

Last time I wrote about people who say they don't have any sense of a need for faith. It's an odd thing to say about something which the Bible presents as wonderful good news. People aren't usually unwilling to accept gifts given in good faith or to decline with "I don't feel any need of that".

And Christianity is all about God's gift of salvation – forgiveness for all our sins, the promise of eternal life in His heaven, and in the present a sense of purpose for living in good times and bad.

I love the story of a Christmas custom in one country where parents decide what is to be the main gift for each child. It is then bound round with wool or string. The next most precious gift is then held against the bundle and more wool is wrapped round it. So it goes on to eventually form what is called a Wonder Ball. Can you imagine the excitement on Christmas morning when the wool is unravelled and they discover one gift after another, each one better than the one before.

It's true that Jesus makes demands too (we've thought about that before), but that story illustrates what John meant when he wrote about Christ: "From his fullness we have all received, grace upon grace" (John 1:16).

The idea of not needing faith in Christ kind of misses the point. It's odd to speak about a lack of a sense of need when we're talking about the most wonderful news you could hear. Remember Jesus' story about the pearl merchant who saw a very valuable pearl somewhere and he was prepared to sell all his other possessions in order to buy that very precious one (Matthew 13:45-46). Thankfully, we don't have to sell things or buy anything from God; his gift is a free gift – and how good is that news! It's the gift of forgiveness, joy and eternal life.

Lastly, think of the subject of appetite. A loss of appetite is a sign of illness, isn't it? What would you think of a doctor who said, "Oh, that's OK; if you don't feel like eating, no problem"? There is a problem, and the doctor will try to diagnose it so that it can be treated and you can become healthy again and have a good appetite. The lack of a taste for food doesn't make any difference to our need for food.

With that cheery thought, I'll sign off for now. All the best for the exams.

Grandad

11th December
Dear Sam,

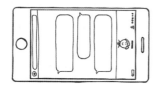

Last time I touched on miracles.

Belief in miracles is another thing that some people regard as a no-no. They say things like, "How can twenty-first century people be expected to believe that Jesus could feed 5,000 people with five loaves and two fish?" I heard of somebody who said he would accept Christianity if the miracles were removed from the Bible; he said the church needs to "get real" if it hopes to win modern people! Whether he *would* believe if all the miracles were removed from the Bible is an interesting question.

It's also interesting to realise that the Bible isn't so full of miracles as people often imagine. It does record many miracles, but they tend to occur at particular periods and it has been estimated (I've never tried to check this out) that if they were averaged out in the period covered by the Bible, there would be roughly a miracle every thirty years; some people might even have lived their whole lives without seeing one.

But what is a miracle? Never mind the jokey use of the word – like saying it would be a miracle if you and your sister could get along for a whole week without any arguments. But let's think about certain things about miracles:

• Sometimes miracles in the Bible are miracles of timing, like the Israelites crossing the Red Sea. Exodus 14:21 says, "The LORD drove the sea back by a strong east wind all night" so that the escapees could cross over. The Bible gives that explanation, but how amazing that it happened at just that moment. Coincidence? Hardly.

• There are other "ordinary" miracles that only seem ordinary because we take them for granted. A poet called John Donne suggested that there are many things which would seem miracles if they didn't happen every day. From the working of the brain to the growing of grain, miracles are all around us.

• And then there are the occasions when the normal laws of nature are overcome, as when Jesus (and Peter) walked on the water (Matthew 14:25-33). One approach is to try to explain it away – suggesting, for example, that there was a sandbank just below the surface and gullible people just thought Jesus was walking on the water. But Bible people weren't fools, and it isn't right to have a closed mind about what may or may not happen. John Lennox, who is a Professor of Maths at Oxford and who knows a thing or two about science, has said that the rejection of the supernatural in principle is unscientific and irrational.

• And the other thing about miracles is that we are talking about Almighty God. It is God who is the Creator of everything that exists and the question is, "Is anything too difficult for God?" (Genesis 18:14)

Now – thinking cap time again. Here's a conundrum to think about: does belief in miracles lead to faith in God or does faith in God lead to belief in miracles?

When we read the New Testament we find that miracles often didn't lead to faith, and also that Jesus refused to perform miracles in response to challenges like: "The Pharisees came and began to argue with him, seeking from him a sign from heaven to test him." (Mark 8:11) Miracles were intended as "signs" (that's John's word for them), but Jesus wouldn't simply satisfy the demand for something spectacular.

Sometimes people will say, "Why don't miracles happen today?" Or they might say that the reason they don't believe is that they prayed for a miracle to cure a loved one and it didn't happen. Well, we can't just order God about. He has His reasons for the things He allows to happen, even if it may be only after this life is over that we see the full picture.

And "after this life is over" brings us to the greatest miracle of all. If Jesus really rose from the dead, then that grand miracle may help us to accept other miraculous things.

A friend of mine went to see the film, *The Greatest Story Ever Told*. The film builds up to a climax with Jesus' crucifixion, and my friend said that there was complete silence for a few moments and then he heard the sound of seats tipping up as people got up to leave – as if the film was finished. But it didn't finish there. At Easter that same Jesus came back to them. And you could say that the whole of Christianity depends on the fact of Jesus' resurrection

Around Easter we thought about the evidence for it, even though it's beyond our limited understanding. It has been said that the gospels don't explain the resurrection; the resurrection explains the gospels.

And maybe you've heard of the High Court judge who wrote in a letter: "As a lawyer I have made a prolonged study of the evidences for the events of the first Easter Day. To me the evidence is conclusive, and over and over again in the High Court I have secured the verdict on evidence not nearly so compelling… As a lawyer I accept the Gospel evidence for the resurrection unreservedly."

However, it's nearly Christmas, not Easter. And we'll be singing about miraculous events, because Christmas isn't just about the joy that comes "when a child is born". It's about the joy that came into the world because that Child was born.

And before finishing, I'd like to refer to a man who taught a Bible Class for about fifty years. He was asked once why he had given so much time and attention to it, and his reply was: "So that every boy (it was a Boys' Brigade Bible Class) might have a Bible in his hands, that he might have a Saviour in his heart, that he might have a purpose in his life". That's a great goal, and if you have these things you are truly rich: a Bible in your hands, a Saviour in your heart and a purpose in your life.

I suppose you know Garfield, the cartoon cat (when I say "know" – well, you know what I mean). In one cartoon Garfield says, "All I do is eat and sleep. Eat and sleep. Eat and sleep. There must be more to a cat's life than that. But I hope not." Well, whatever we say about cats, there's meant to be more of a sense of purpose in a human life, and it's Jesus who said that trusting and following Him is the way to "have life and have it abundantly." (John 10:10)

I expect you'll be busy over the next few weeks (with parties and shopping), but Granny and I are really looking forward to coming to your house for Christmas dinner. We hope to arrive in time to go to church with you, and then – well, bring on the turkey!

We made a New Year resolution to exchange letters through the year, and we've kept it up! What shall we write about next year?

Love to all
Grandad

THE AUTHOR: David J Randall is a retired minister who lives near Broughty Ferry. He continues preaching and writing, and also enjoys running and swimming. He and his wife have six grandchildren.

BIBLIOGRAPHY: *If I Had Faked the Resurrection*, Josh McDowell, published in April 2000 edition of magazine of *Focus on the Family*
The New Testament in Modern English, J B Phillips, Geoffrey Bles (London), 1960
Prince Caspian, The Chronicles of Narnia, Geoffrey Bles (London) 1951
A Lifetime of Wisdom, Joni Eareckson, Zondervan, 2009
Why I am Not an Atheist, David J. Randall, 2016, Christian Focus Publications, ISBN: 978-1-78191-270-6